Journal of the Architects Regional Council Asia (ARCASIA)

T0272236

Contents

Editorial

The long-standing and enduring historical and cultural stamps of Asian countries form a characteristic architecture heritage and shape a distinctive historical heritage in the old urban quarters of these countries. Taking the professional responsibility to respect history as they face the future, and with the understanding of indigenous cultures in Asian countries, contemporary Asian architects use different approaches to explore new methods of combining historic architecture and blocks with cities brimming with modern life. In their practice and exploration of renovation, the usually contradictory notions projected by catchwords like "renovation and regeneration," "materials and spirit," "hardware and software," and "tradition and modern" become synonyms. These words and the sentiments they attach continually evolve and combine under various environmental, cultural, and technological conditions, forming a future-oriented innovation of ideas and methods. In this issue, enlightening discussions on the issue's theme of Renovation and Innovation unfold in three academic articles and eleven design projects.

In the three academic essays, the discussion emerges from three aspects: historic building conservation, the revitalization process of these historic buildings, and the regeneration of historic old urban quarters. In "The Concept of Sharing and Regeneration in Contemporary Architecture in Pakistan: A Case Study of Har Sukh Mansion," Amna Iqbal analyzes the conservation of Har Sukh Mansion in Pakistan, including environmental, social, and cultural sustainability issues, arguing that the interconnection of renovation, design, as well as cultural and environmental studies should be emphasized in the renovation and regeneration of historic architecture. In the second essay "Beyond (Designing) the Place," based on the revitalization of the former Haw Par Mansion and Tiger Balm Garden (the property's private garden) in Hong Kong into Haw Par Music, Wu Tsan Sum Roger explains that the revitalization of a building encompasses not only the renovation of the "hardware" of that building, but also the inheritance and innovation of its "software" programs. The author explains this concept in detail on pages 13 to 24. The final essay in the lineup discusses a revitalization and regeneration process that extends beyond a single building to a whole neighborhood filled with heritage architecture and historical heritage. Taking the old urban quarter in Yingping District in Xiamen, China, as an example, the authors discuss—through the multiple dimensions of the protection of local culture, improvement of environment, creation of public space, and improvement of infrastructure—sharing and regeneration strategies for old urban quarters in Asia.

On the practice side, architectural practices Neri&Hu along with K2LD, HGAA, and Nikken Sekkei share how the traditional housing prototype combines with the modern lifestyle to create a restrained and serene space atmosphere. A wholly different approach is revealed by IROJE KHM Architects, who interpret a rich and lively contemporary settlement scene with exaggerated architecture. MIKAMI Architects and Oshida Architects & Engineers explore the transplantation of local attachment in public architecture, while OPEN Architecture and Tongji Architectural Design explore two completely different solutions to the merging of architecture and landscape with the natural environment in three eco-positive, remarkable projects. HAS Design and Research addresses the twofold problem of space and society by exploring innovative materials, at the same time attaching cultural significance to them. TSC Architects and Tanzo Space Design Office create bright and healthy atmospheres through materials and space in the hope of changing the depressing and constrained stereotypes of certain familiar architecture types, like clinics/hospitals.

In these engaging projects, the design practices featured in this issue provide unique responses to the idea "traditional innovation and innovational tradition."

The Concept of Sharing and Regeneration in Contemporary Architecture in Pakistan
A Case Study of Har Sukh Mansion

Amna IQBAL, Assistant Professor, Superior University, Lahore, Pakistan
Asma ASLAM, Lecturer, Superior University, Lahore, Pakistan
Farhana RASHEED, Assistant Professor, Superior University, Lahore, Pakistan
Umer MALIK, Assistant Professor, Superior University, Lahore, Pakistan

Abstract

The challenges that face the design and planning of a sustainable built environment include human health, insufficient resources, climate variations, carbon footprint, and urbanization. Given this, regenerative architecture may play a vital role in creating a net positive impact on the environment. The work of landscape architect Ian McHarg, who published the book *Design with Nature* in 1969, laid the groundwork for regenerative development and design. McHarg invented a method for ecological land use planning that was based on the knowledge of natural systems.

The ultimate goal of regenerative development is to redesign systems with absolute effectiveness that permit the co-evolution of the human species and other species, while the highest goal of sustainable development is to meet today's basic human needs without compromising the ability of future generations to meet theirs.

In this research, the distinctive traits of the architectural style of Kamil Khan Mumtaz in his Har Sukh Mansion, a regenerative architecture, are discussed, focusing on the unique amalgamation of contemporary and traditional architecture. Among Kamil's projects, Har Sukh Mansion is the most successful contemporary example of traditional architecture. This paper explores the beautifully designed external fabric and interior space planning of the building, highlighting its regenerative ancient haveli architectural style.

The principle of sharing is applied artistically by integrating private residential and public institutional areas within the building complex, while maintaining privacy through internal segregation. Two methodologies were employed to assess the mansion's regenerative impact: The first was a critical investigation of the complex's interior and outdoor areas based on the principle of sharing and regeneration; and the second was a qualitative research approach that involved conducting expert interviews based on a set of questions that assess the architecture's impact. This mansion is evaluated to be one of the best examples of sustainably designed buildings based on its massive structure and the use of lime plaster, which minimizes the building's carbon footprint, while regulating the temperature of the interior.

Author Information
Amna IQBAL: amna.iqbal@superior.edu.pk
Asma ASLAM: asmaaslam@superior.edu.pk
Farhana RASHEED: farhana.rasheed@superior.edu.pk
Umer MALIK: umer.malik@superior.edu.pk

Keywords

Sharing, resources, regenerative architecture style, traditional architecture, environment, sustainable, space planning, development.

1. Introduction

Throughout the history of human civilization, cycles of degeneration, transformation, integration, and utilization of buildings have been common factors of the built environment. Conventionally, architectural theorists have been authoritarian in their conclusions—be it Vitruvius highlighting classical architecture in the first century CE (Common Era), or Le Corbusier praising modernism in the twentieth century CE. Only lately, architecture is being envisioned beyond perception and method-driven approaches because of a collective move toward postmodern ideas.[1]

Typical building design and construction methods have a devastating effect on the environment. These issues cannot be fully explored in the current era of contemporary society's development along the concept of sustainable design and development—the purpose of which is to create fewer environmental damage—so, as a result, the concept of regeneration is gaining traction as it shifts the current construction paradigm toward a more human-centric approach.[2]

The construction industry is being highlighted as one of the main contributors to environmental deprivation and one of the main reasons for climate change at 50 percent depletion of resources, and consumption of energy at 40 percent.[3] The majority of structures are constructed using non-sustainable methods that disregard human needs and the natural environment. The conventional way of construction contributes almost 40 percent of global energy consumption and nearly 36 percent of CO_2 emissions.[4] Over the last few decades, the idea of sustainability is being promoted in contemporary architectural practices, focusing on the fulfillment of present societal needs, as well as the demands of future generations. For a less harmful impact on the environment, the regulatory principles are based on the amalgamation of social, environmental, and economic aspects.[5]

Considering cities as the core of diversity, their existing fabric and constant evolution to cater to the ever-changing needs and fashions of its residents are significant dominant traits. "Regeneration," as defined by Peter Roberts is "a widespread and integrated vision for resolving the problems related to the built environment," and pursues to bring a lasting change in economic, social, physical, and environmental conditions of an area.[6] One of the guiding norms of regeneration projects is based on creating an icon as a focal point for the new community.

Andrew Tallon discusses two theoretical keystones of regeneration that seem to be contradictory, but often work side by side. One of the first ideas of the Enlightenment (Age of Reason)—universalism and citizens' right to well-being and a healthy environment—was later recreated through post–World War II Keynesian influences for the welfare society, and more recently, in the United Nations' Sustainable Development Goals.[7] The second theoretical perspective is neoliberalism, which promotes the entrepreneurial model of urban growth and management above the municipal model. Because of these entrepreneurial dynamics, the key player position shifts from reacting and monitoring to recognizing regeneration objectives. These theories claim that architecture and place have transformative power and may be used to ameliorate socioeconomic conditions.

The design of a building does not end after it is constructed; it is an ongoing process, but its use is determined by the activities of the residents and landlords.[8] Hence, it is not surprising that

architectural regeneration, with its inherent flexibility, diversity, and multiplicity, emerged throughout the postmodern period. Today, architectural regeneration discovers itself in an era where disciplinary constraints are diminishing. Depending on their function, various people may use buildings at different durations in their life cycle. The use of a building is not a continuous phase, but rather a series of events that occur over time. Buildings may be occupied, reorganized, uninhibited, reoccupied, extended, renovated, and scaled in variations during their life span.[9]

Architectural regeneration primarily intersects with theories of utility and overabundance within the design theory domain. In functional theories, the form is related to function, emphasizing that once the function is detached, the building becomes redundant, but the functionality can evolve and may define a new function based on artistic process. All buildings, ultimately, turn dysfunctional.[10] The form is somewhat predefined in the process of regeneration, however, it can be changed and the persona can be transformed with a new function.

Ian Morrison and Merlin Waterson provide a fresh viewpoint regarding regeneration, emphasizing the need for built-in flexibility as a key feature for easy adaptability and long-term extent of the building life cycle.[11] A planned action of renewal with anticipated economic and social advantages is a process of regeneration. Buildings are innately connected to their built environments. As buildings are refurbished, so, too, are the surrounding neighborhoods, resulting in changes to the area, which eventually affect the individual buildings, their utilization, maintenance, and their land economic value.[12]

The notion of place identification, in light of regeneration theory, refers to how physical, emotional, and mystical connection to a place strengthens the sense of community and belonging among its inhabitants. Regeneration projects are generally sensitive to the local sense of place, for instance, building form, street pattern, construction materials, and socio-economic practices.[13] Economic gains can be obtained in a variety of ways: through a good, suited fit with the locally distinct characteristic style, or through the process of architectural branding, which plays an important role.

In the Indian subcontinent, cultural dualism—which is a product of the century-long British rule in its history—influenced the dynamics of the societies in various states following independence in 1947. This paved the way for a contemporary cultural dialogue in Pakistan, in which the conflicting cultural demands for modernity and tradition emerged as a central issue; but individual feelings of architects, builders, and clients influenced how the concepts of modernity and tradition were applied to architecture.[14] Pakistan's people have had a million years to build a culture with many ethnic groupings. Pakistan's architectural identity is shaped by a million years of cultural evolution, human behavior, ideals, and technology.

According to architect Kamil Khan Mumtaz, the West has taken a stance on modern architecture based on historical experience, and has aligned with the philosophy after comprehending it. However, many architects in Pakistan have replicated this work without paying sufficient consideration to Pakistan's national style, available technology, and local building and planning techniques. It should be noted that architects are not only responsible for the state of architecture in cities such as Lahore and Karachi; if the customer is rich enough, they can without difficulty gather examples from all over the globe and then order the architect to include those components and styles based on the client's preferences rather than on the design's merit. This trend/practice and both the clients' and architects' different approaches have jointly harmed city architecture and the built environment.[15]

As the region grew, Pakistan developed a rich architectural history. However, three major periods of architecture appear to have affected Pakistan's overall architectural realm: Mughal architecture, British architecture, and contemporary architecture. For practicing architects like Kamil, the revived review of Islamic architectural traditions, as well as the quest for a modern architectural expression were found in large concerns mostly in building and construction in embryonic nationstates.[16]

Kamil is one of Pakistan's regenerative and vernacular architects working to construct structures that are more climate sensitive, concentrating on passive design for human comfort, resulting in a greater net beneficial influence on the environment. His architectural practices reflect the continuation of tradition in contemporary style, which is considered as being wiped out from current building practices. The purpose of this paper is to assess the regeneration potential of one of Kamil Sahab's buildings, Har Sukh Mansion. "Progress" on the way to "enlightenment" was traditionally used to assess human "development." The purpose of art in traditional civilizations has been to assist this spiritual search or journey by reminding us of our place and function in this life, pointing to our real goal and illuminating the path to that goal. Traditional and modern ideas about growth and what it is to be human represent two completely contradictory worldviews. For millennia, the ancient worldview defined our humanity and maintained our environment, but the contemporary development paradigm has driven all of humanity and life on our planet to the verge of extinction.[17]

The use of indigenous building materials and technologies with low carbon footprints, economic sustainability, and social relevance demanded study, experimentation, and tests of indigenous building materials and structural forms. The materials of choice for foundations, bearing walls, arches, and roofs in Central Punjab were determined to be burnt clay bricks and lime mortar.[18] This has resulted in the revival of "lost" dome-building constructions such as flat and ribbed domes, as well as muqarnas, which were constructed without the use of Portland cement, reinforcing steel, or shuttering. Visual languages, symbolic forms, and aesthetic notions support the worldview or ideological framework that all traditional civilizations are built on. For millennia, these are the cultures that have preserved humankind and the environment.

1.1 Principles of Architectural Regeneration

1.1.1 Architecture as a Cultural Process
Any location or building, be it historical or modern, or urban or rural, is inextricably related to the people who design, create, live in, or who are in any other way connected to it (visitors or neighbors), as well as its surroundings. Changes in the environment, communities, and cultures they represent, whether spatial, material, or functional, occur inexorably through time and are followed by modest to major social, economic, and political consequences. A credit to this procedural character of the architecture and its connection with the cultural values, society, and environment is the core of architectural regeneration.[19] The objective of regeneration is to create a

lively future constructed environment that balances past and present, and tradition and modernity, for an impending fluid, fast-changing, and unpredictable world, in addition to improving architectural and socioeconomic conditions.

1.1.2 Context/Environment Matters
Conservation theories and principles consider buildings as a discrete element in a location, rather than a complicated system of socio-economic, environmental, physical, and historical networks. Any intervention or modification will affect the context of the building. Architectural regeneration is a complex process that does not happen in a vacuum, but is influenced by the past legacy and present built environment or future targets, and also by the broader social, cultural, and economic condition that they are a part of.[20]

1.1.3 Adaptive Capacity and Robustness
Adaptive capacity refers to the ability of a building to adapt to changing applications and requirements. It is defined as "the ability of a space to adapt to different utilizations without any considerable change to its physical features."[21] Adaptive capacity is linked to the robustness of the space and the capacity of a building or space to be altered while withstanding its architectural, historical, and cultural value. An architecturally and functionally robust building can be a more cost-effective option when it comes to adaptation.

1.1.4 Contextual Complexity and Interconnectedness
Architectural regeneration is a multidisciplinary endeavor that aims to not only identify multiple values associated with a place, but also to make functional adaptations to the building, improve its environment, and increase its ability to adapt.[22] So, the built environment is more like a system instead of a set plan, with the continuous revolution of buildings within it. Flexibility and interconnection, according to Bie Plevoets and Koenraad Van Cleempoel, has become an academic and practical topic that crosses the scales of the interior, architecture, and planning, as well as economic, ecological, cultural, and social problems.[23]

1.1.5 Resource Efficiency and Management
The Living Building Challenge standards (LBC) endeavor to transform the conventional construction standard and methodology for the design and construction of buildings toward creating a net positive impact on the built environment, lifestyles, and cultural norms of our human communities.[24] The water and sanitation system of buildings to be constructed can be developed with technology that is reasonably simple to maintain, and which meets LBC requirements. The water system can be based on collecting rainwater in tanks, which entirely satisfies the building's water needs. Rainwater may be cleansed using an ultraviolet (UV) system and used in the bathrooms and kitchen.[25]

Within the scope of this research, a case study of an existing residential building was also conducted; this building is certified as the first regenerative building in Spain. It is located in the small village of Bresca, 850 meters above sea level, on the top of a hill overlooking a river nearby and surrounding mountains. In this building, the drinking water is filtered separately in a smaller tank with an active carbon filter and mineral stones that supplement the filtered, collected rainwater with minerals. In comparison to the 150 liters consumed in a conventionally planned dwelling, the total interior daily water usage per person in this regenerative building has been lowered to 50 liters. The wetland section is made up of an outdoor area with gravel and plants which use greywater from showers, sinks, and the kitchen, which is treated, collected, and stored for irrigation. Photovoltaic panels installed on the roof share the electricity load, making the building more sustainable and regenerative.[26]

1.1.6 Building Materials and Regenerative Space Planning

The carbon emissions of building materials are taken into account throughout their life cycle, beginning with their manufacture, construction, usage, and demolition or reuse/recycling. As a result, construction materials in a building are quite important. A passive design technique can be employed to incorporate wood fiber thermal insulation in the outside walls, roof, and floor to meet regenerative building imperatives.[27]

In this first regenerative building of Spain, there are two styles of rendering on the outer walls. The initial depiction is made out of natural clay and sand plaster. The second form includes radiant tubes made of clay and straw. Competent craftspeople were needed to produce such a rendering, which was completed by a local team that specialized in these techniques. Another example of a stacking function in this building is the use of a clay and straw finish. This method allows for the use of local materials and ensures a very biophilic aesthetic and tactile result, a large thermal mass, and an improvement in the wall's radiant impact.[28] Adding to that, the material is also of low cost. An airtight barrier was also installed in the external walls behind the inner masonry. Spain's imperative living economy-sourcing requirement states that 20 percent of the materials must come from within 500 kilometers of the building's site, 30 percent from within 1,000 kilometers, 25 percent from within 5,000 kilometers, and 25 percent from anywhere, while the consultants must come from within 2,500 kilometers.

By studying the internal planning of this first regenerative building in Spain, it is observed that the interior spaces are planned according to passive design principles, where most spaces of maximum utilization are oriented to the south, being a prime orientation for passive solar heating based on the site location. The utility spaces are arranged along the north of the building, thus minimizing energy loss. The use of fruit trees and other types of vegetation that provide different benefits to the building's inhabitants reflects the building's ecological design policy, which means various design components perform multiple functions, providing biophilic aspects to the building. The project utilizes the principle of natural ventilation for cooling the indoor air by convection and evapotranspiration to maintain high efficiency and a regenerative character in every climatic condition.[29]

2. Methodology

This study aims to look at the design parameters, materials, procedures, and technologies used in the design and construction of regenerative buildings in Pakistan, whichever the region. The contemporary architecture of Pakistan—considering different climatic regions have their local materials and construction methodologies—aids in the development of the vernacular architecture of any region. To evaluate the regenerative influence of a project, two approaches were used. One was a qualitative research methodology that used expert interviews with two stakeholders to obtain a direct assessment by professionals within the context of regenerative projects and sustainable development;

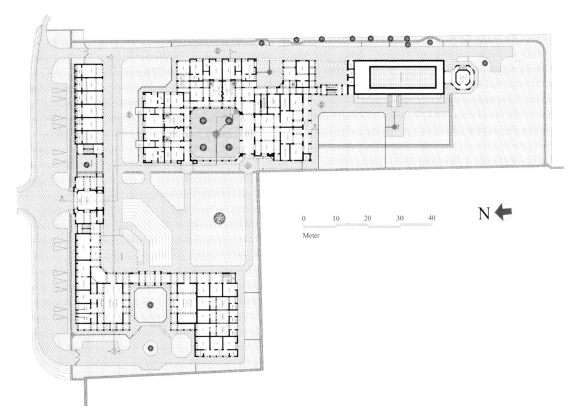

0   10   20   30   40
Meter

N ◀

Figure 1
Ground-floor plan,
Har Sukh Mansion

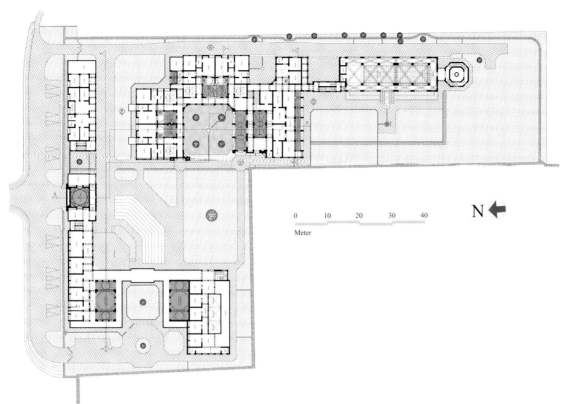

Figure 2
First-floor plan, Har Sukh
Mansion

the expert interviews were held based on several questions that evaluated the impact of these projects. The other methodology was a critical analysis of the interior and exterior spaces of the complex based on the concept of sharing and regeneration.

2.1 Har Sukh Mansion—A Residential Community and Organic Farm Complex

To illustrate the application of these principles in this study, Kamil's Har Sukh Mansion is used as a case study. It is a residential community and organic farm complex located at Theater Village, off Bedian Road. The complex features a haveli design and includes a family residence for the parents; suites for four children; working and teaching studios for art, dance, and music; a library, amphitheater, and swimming pool; garages; and housing for visiting scholars (Figure 1, page 7; Figure 2).

2.1.1 Cultural Relevance in the Architecture of Har-Sukh Mansion

Reflecting ideal forms with embedded meanings relating to the metaphysical worldview, architectural forms and spatial order promote the feeling of place and history in any building. Traditional arts and crafts had a strong link to the metaphysical and idealist worldview that all traditional cultures shared. The artist or craftsperson cannot claim to be "original"—except in the sense of returning to one's roots— or claim to "create" beauty within this framework. Out there, as an objective reality, beauty already exists. The artist can only hope that his/her art reflects this beauty in its design (Figure 3, Figure 4).

In Har Sukh Mansion, the ideal forms, as well as their elements and ornamentation, can be read as a language of symbols, with meanings that are either implicit—as in

architectural elements, geometric patterns, floral or other natural motifs—or explicit—as in iconographic sculpture and painting, but more often in calligraphy in Islamic art and architecture (Figure 5).

Proportioning and the usage of "ideal forms" are two fundamental elements of classical design methods used in the complex. To comprehend the significance of copying—both as a means of design and as a method of instruction—one must first comprehend the essential role of "ideal forms" in traditional aesthetic theory, as well as the creative process within conventional worldview and cosmology.

Traditionally, the term "art" has been used to refer to all forms of art and craft. In reality, it may be applied to anything that satisfies the dual criterion of function and aesthetics. Now, utility pertains to quantity and the more obvious practical and physical aspects of material and form, such as suitability for function and purpose. However, beauty is linked to quality, and it is usually seen as a Divine quality. Everything in the created universe, according to classical cosmology, is a manifestation of the Divine (Figure 6, page 10).

2.1.2 Context and Environmental Sensitivity

Simple design principles and elements for climate and comfort, including verandas for air movement, orientation, thermal capacity, shading, courtyards, and evaporative cooling (ducted air from rooftop desert coolers) are incorporated into the design of the building complex. Indigenous plants, water, and marine fauna and aquatic plants in the oxidation pond integrate residential land uses with agriculture and organic farming to form a sustainable mini ecosystem.

The composite climate of Lahore requires three distinct responses: open-to-sky courtyards and roof terraces for hot, dry

Figure 3
Front elevation of Har Sukh
Mansion

Figure 4
Institutional unit of Har Sukh
Mansion

summer nights and winter days; semi-open verandas and a *barsati* (a habitable room on the roof of a building that may or may not include a kitchen and toilet) that allow for maximum air movement during the warm, humid monsoon season; and enclosed spaces with high thermal capacity to combat hot, dry summer days and winter nights.

2.1.3 Robustness in Hur Sukh Mansion
Privacy and a hierarchy of public and private spaces are culturally relevant design elements that are incorporated within a building's space planning. The complex layout is usually planned such that it avoids "distancing" between artist, craftsperson, producer, and product; hence, segregating the residential and institutional enclosures along with their outdoor spaces (Figure 7, page 11).

2.1.4 Resource Management
Crucial to this project was the unreserved support of the builders, Messrs Maymar, not only in the form of time, work force, and materials, but also with their professional knowledge of material sciences and structural engineering. The contractor fully embraced the design philosophy and approach and responded with enthusiasm to find imaginative solutions to many technical challenges.

Various passive design strategies have been adapted in the building design, thereby relying less on mechanical resources. Photovoltaic cells are installed on the roof, with a backup generator as a supplement to the public power grid; baths and kitchens are designed with passive water heating; for cooking, biogas from kitchens and animal waste is used. Wood burning fireplaces for space heating have been installed to avoid electric

Figure 5
Interior views of Har Sukh
Mansion

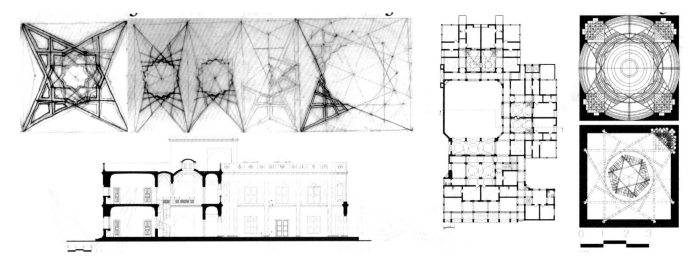

Figure 6
Geometrical and classical
elements of Har Sukh
Mansion

or gas heaters; surface and wastewater is collected through open
channels and directed to the anaerobic and aerobic treatment
plant; and farm irrigation is supplemented with an effluent
storage pond and water recycling.

2.1.5 Building Materials and Construction Techniques
Indigenous materials have a low ecological footprint, low
embedded energy in their processing and manufacture, and are
economically sustainable. In the construction of this complex, the
consideration was to avoid high embedded energy materials, such
as cement, steel, and aluminum, and to minimize the use of glass,
instead using sheesham wood, neem wood, brick, kankar (detrital
rolled calcium carbonate formed in soil), terra cotta clay tiles,
white lime mortar, and plaster. Low-tech construction methods use
manual rather than mechanical methods of construction, including
flat domes and muqarnas without shuttering.

Structural forms, including domes, vaults, and arches were
designed in the complex. Reviving traditional techniques and forms,
such as flat domes, ribbed domes, and muqarnas within the
building make up another benchmark in vernacular architecture.

2.1.6 Heritage Conservation
Any policy on the conservation of cultural heritage would be
meaningless unless it is linked to a strategy for the survival of
humanity and the environment. To achieve such a policy, we must
begin with a redefinition of development itself—its goals and
objectives concerning what it means to be human. Har Sukh
Mansion is one of the best expressions of heritage
conservation achieved through architectural character,
building materials, and construction techniques.

2.2 Interviews with the Stakeholders
Various interviews were conducted with multiple stakeholders of the
building, including regeneration and conservation experts, and the
client, Madam Bina Jawad, to gather their sentiments on whether
the concept of sharing and regeneration is successfully being
adopted within the building.

2.2.1 Interview with the Client
As shared by Madam Bina Jawad during the interview, she had
initiated with the plan of an eco-friendly residence on the
family's farm for herself, her husband, three married daughters,
and a son. The Jawad Khawaja family includes musicians,
dancers, and painters who needed studios and ancillary
facilities such as garages, grain stores, staff quarters, and
utilities. These requirements were added to during the design
stage to include an amphitheater, accommodation for visiting
artists, a swimming pool, water reservoir, pump house, and
sewage treatment plant. At present, some spaces have been
converted to serve uses not originally intended, in order to
support the sharing quality of regenerative architecture; for
example, the staff quarters have become apartments for visiting
artists, and the music facility and library are being used as
temporary classrooms for a primary school. Throughout the
project, the core concerns of the client were low cost, energy
efficiency, and water conservation.

Madam Jawad further explained that the family is passionate
about their commitment to traditional arts, organic farming, and
sustainable living, which complemented the architect's quest for an
architecture responsive to climate, and appropriate to the social
and economic realities of our time. This interview leads to the

conclusion that the regenerative principle of adaptive capacity of a building is very well integrated in the mansion.

2.2.2 Interview with the Experts
For the evaluation by conservation and regeneration experts, interviews were done based on the following criteria:
· The reintroduction of traditional architectural character in the contemporary context of the present day.
· The incorporation of Mughal architectural features in a complex of residential and institutional units.
· The importance of heritage conservation for developing a sense of belonging and regeneration for net positive impact in the field of architecture.

The high-profile interview panel included the highly respected and revered Sir Pervaiz Vandal, who founded the Trust for History of Art and Architecture in Pakistan (THAAP) and who has been conducting public interest lectures and organizing the THAAP annual international conferences in Pakistan since 2010. Sir Vandal heads an architectural practice in partnership with Professor Sajida Vandal named Pervaiz Vandal & Associates. In 2016, the Commonwealth Association of Architects (CAA) jointly awarded the 2016 Sir Robert Mathew Award for excellence in architecture to the British firm Grimshaw Architects and Pervaiz Vandal & Associates. A second interview was conducted with Madam Fauzia Qureshi, Director of FHQ & Associates (SMC-PVT) Ltd. As a private consultant, Madam Qureshi has to date been engaged in the planning and conservation of the environment and, more specifically, the built heritage and architectural design of educational, institutional, commercial, and residential buildings, as well as their interior design. She authored the policy document for the National Heritage and Culture Division in 1988 for the purposes of heritage conservation in Pakistan, and has also prepared conservation and management plans for three of the World Heritage sites of Pakistan: Lahore Fort (2003), Shalimar Gardens (2006), and Rohtas Fort (2006).

According to the opinion of both Sir Vandal and Madam Qureshi, current day presents a high time for the need to conserve Pakistan's heritage in the contemporary context to meet the demands of sustainability and regeneration, given that the land's indigenous materials and traditional architectural style are the best fit to the culture and climate of the region. The use of traditional architectural elements and locally available materials don't only afford suitability to the built environment, but also help to develop a sense of belonging to the community, which has sorely been ignored in following the contemporary trends of the West (Europe and the United Kingdom) that present as misfits in Pakistan's climate, and which demand an increased reliance on mechanical means for thermal comfort.

They further explained that the international style that has been followed for decades needs to finally be disowned and that now would be the time to embrace our socio-cultural norms and traditional architecture to have a net positive impact on the environment. The utilization of Mughal architectural elements in a residential complex was a unique initiative by Mumtaz; before, it was only used in developing monumental and royal buildings like forts, palaces, and great mosques during the time of the Mughal Empire. The architect has beautifully incorporated traditional Mughal architectural elements into the contemporary context, resulting in an exemplary built form that houses residential and institutional buildings within one complex. The experts endorse

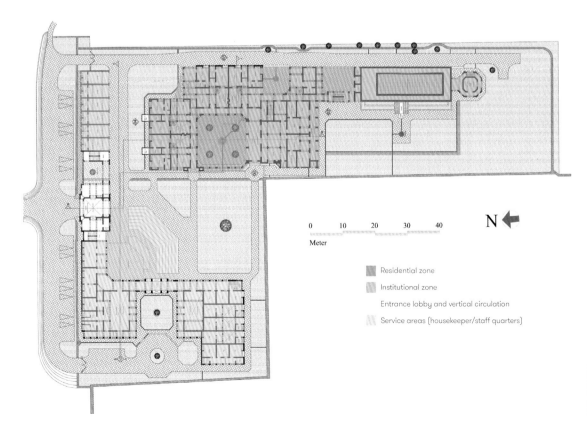

0 10 20 30 40
Meter

N ⬅

Residential zone

Institutional zone

Entrance lobby and vertical circulation

Service areas (housekeeper/staff quarters)

Figure 7
Layout of functional zoning—Har Sukh Mansion

the architect for his conviction and efforts (despite challenges faced) in finding the trained craftspeople familiar with and capable of delivering the intricacies required by this work; it would have been demanding to develop such meticulous and complicated geometries, muqarnas, ribbed domes, stuccos, and various other elements with such precision.

The experts also highlighted the successful incorporation of the concept of sharing in this project, which creates a complex that houses residential units along with institutional units for cultural arts and crafts. The spaces are segregated finely in the building planning and layout, yet are still all connected, reflecting a single complex. In the experts' conclusion, Har Sukh Mansion is a fine example of regenerative architecture and more buildings should be developed following this example to represent Pakistan's rich cultural and architectural traits, which are the best fit for the region's built environment, and which cause the least harm to the environment.

3. Conclusion

Architectural regeneration refers to the process of repurposing, adapting, and evolving existing structures in an urban or rural setting in ways that take into account the effects that these decisions and interventions have on the regeneration of a place, and are guided by principles of environmental, social, and cultural sustainability. This paper and its discussion reveal how concepts of architecture, design, conservation, regeneration, cultural studies and environmental studies are all interconnected. These ideas impact architectural regeneration; they borrows, modify, and eventually contribute to its progress.

More significantly, though, the research shows that architectural regeneration is a dynamic and complicated process that not only deals with physical and empirical factors, but also has an influence on social, cultural, and environmental settings.

Architectural regeneration is thus guided by a set of principles that overlap with those that guide design, conservation, environmental and social activities, while also placing architectural regeneration in its own realm. Architectural, spatial, environmental, economic, and social circumstances all influence the reuse and regeneration of existing built environments, which is part of a continual cultural process. Through physical processes of addition and subtraction, a building's or area's tangible and intangible adaptive capacity informs its potential to change and be transformed while preserving architectural and social values, and meanings. Architectural regeneration is inter-scalar, in that it occurs in many sizes, ranging from the interiors of buildings to entire cities, and in such a way that a change at one scale necessarily affects changes at others. Ultimately, creativity and innovative approaches to design, functionality, and financing are what drive the success of architectural regeneration.

Despite the relevance of architectural regeneration, the high upfront expenditure hampers the frequent development of regenerative buildings. The prices of new plumbing systems, PV panels, and, notably, energy storage systems are constantly rising due to inflation. To address this issue and encourage the adoption of the regenerative idea, the government and local governments must develop an incentive structure. This paper concludes that building design based on regenerative architecture should be encouraged and policies should be made for creating a regenerative net positive built environment.

Notes

1. Philip Plowright, *Revealing Architectural Design: Methods, Frameworks and Tools* (United Kingdom: Routledge 2014).
2. Aleksandar Atanas Petrovski, Emmanuel Pauwels, and Aránzazu Galán González, "Implementing Regenerative Design Principles: A Refurbishment Case Study of the First Regenerative Building in Spain," *Sustainability* 13, no. 4 (2021): 2,411.
3. Abdeen Mustafa Omer, "Energy, Environment, and Sustainable Development," *Renewable and Sustainable Energy Review* 12, no. 9: 2,265–3,000.
4. Dejan Mumovic and Mat Santamouris, eds., *A Handbook of Sustainable Building Design and Engineering: An Integrated Approach to Energy, Health, and Operational Performance* (London, United Kingdom: Routledge, 2018).
5. José Cartelle Barros, *Assessing and Optimizing the Sustainability Objective of Electricity Generation Systems, and Energy Systems of Special Interest to Galicia,* doctoral thesis, 2018, Universidade da Coruña.
6. Peter Roberts, "The Evolution, Definition, and Purpose of Urban Regeneration," *Urban Regeneration* (2000): 9–36.
7. Andrew Tallon, *Urban Regeneration in the UK* (United Kingdom: Routledge, 2020).
8. Wendy Gunn and Jared Donovan, *Design and Anthropology* (United Kingdom: Routledge, 2016).
9. Daniel Maudlin and Marcel Vellinga, *Consuming Architecture: On the Occupation, Appropriation and Interpretation of Buildings* (United Kingdom: Routledge, 2014).
10. Tom Verebes, *Masterplanning the Adaptive City: Computational Urbanism in the Twenty-first Century* (New York, United States: Routledge, 2013).
11. Ian Morrison and Merlin Waterson, *Rescue and Reuse: Communities, Heritage and Architecture* (London, United Kingdom: RIBA Publishing, 2019).
12. Aylin Orbaşlı, and Marcel Vellinga, "Architectural Regeneration and its Theoretical Context," *Architectural Regeneration* (2020): 1–25.
13. Morrison and Waterson, *Rescue and Reuse: Communities, Heritage and Architecture.*
14. Muiz Ahmed, "Contemporary Built Form in Pakistan: An Analysis of Residences and Urban Areas of Lahore," *Journal of Research in Architecture and Planning* 20, no. 1 (2016): 21–29.
15. Kamil Khan Mumtaz, *Modernity and Tradition: Contemporary Architecture in Pakistan* (United Kingdom: Oxford University Press, 1999).
16. Ammara Maqsood, *The New Pakistani Middle Class* (United Kingdom: Harvard University Press, 2017).
17. Stephen Gaukroger, *The Emergence of a Scientific Culture: Science and the Shaping of Modernity* (Clarendon Press, 2008), 1,210–1,685.
18. Junli Yang and Ibuchim Cyril B Ogunkah, "A multi-criteria Decision Support System for the Selection of Low-cost Green Building Materials and Components," *Journal of Building Construction and Planning Research* 1, no. 4 (2013): 89.
19. Orbaşlı, and Vellinga, "Architectural Regeneration and its Theoretical Context."
20. Heba ElGahani and Raffaello Furlan, "Post-2022 FIFA World Cup in the State of Qatar: Urban Regeneration Strategies for Doha," *Journal of Urban Regeneration and Renewal* 11, no. 4 (2018): 355–370.
21. Nisha A. Fernando, "Open-ended Space: Urban Streets in Different Cultural Contexts" in *Loose Space: Possibility and Diversity in Urban Life,* eds. Karen A. Franck and Quentin Stevens (United Kingdom: Routledge), 54.
22. Pamela Mang and Bill Reed, "Regenerative Development and Design," *Sustainable Built Environments* (2020): 115–141.
23. Bie Plevoets and Koenraad Van Cleempoel, "Adaptive Reuse as an Emerging discipline: An Historic Survey," in *Reinventing Architecture and Interiors: A Socio-political View on Building Adaptation,* ed. Graham Cairns (United Kingdom: Libri Publishing, 2013), 13–32.
24. Kelli A. Kokame, "More Than Just a Glass Face: What Makes a 'Green' or 'Sustainable' Building, Exactly?" Senior thesis for Bachelor of Arts, Pomona College, California, United States, 2017, 176, https://scholarship.claremont.edu/pomona_theses/176.
25. Hana Drdla, "Urban Renewal: Opportunity for Green Innovation in the Face of Climate Change, A Case Study of Toronto Community Housing," a major paper submitted to the Faculty of Environmental Studies in partial fulfillment of the requirements for the degree of Master in Environmental Studies, York University, Toronto, Ontario, Canada, 2016.
26. Petrovski, Pauwels, and González, "Implementing Regenerative Design Principles."
27. Robert Crawford, *Life Cycle Assessment in the Built Environment* (United Kingdom: Routledge, 2011).
28. Petrovski, Pauwels, and González, "Implementing Regenerative Design Principles."
29. ibid.

Figure Credits

Figure 1: Ground-floor plan, Har Sukh Mansion (courtesy of Ar. Kamil Khan Mumtaz – Project Architect).
Figure 2: First-floor plan, Har Sukh Mansion (courtesy of Ar. Kamil Khan Mumtaz – Project Architect).
Figure 3: Front elevation of Har Sukh Mansion (photo credit: R.K. Studio).
Figure 4: Institutional unit of Har Sukh Mansion (photo credit: R.K. Studio).
Figure 5: Interior views of Har Sukh Mansion (photo credit: R.K. Studio).
Figure 6: Geometrical and classical elements of Har Sukh Mansion (courtesy of Ar. Kamil Khan Mumtaz – Project Architect).
Figure 7: Layout of functional zoning, Har-Sukh Mansion (author's diagram).

Beyond (Designing) the Place

WU Tsan Sum Roger, Executive Director (Project Development), Haw Par Music
Member, Hong Kong Institute of Architects
Member, Royal Institute of British Architects

Abstract

Even with my years of architectural experience working on heritage buildings internationally, it was a real privilege, and tremendously rewarding and thought-provoking to be directly involved in the project to revitalize the former Haw Par Mansion—a Chinese eclectic style residence built by Aw Boon Haw in the 1930s—and its private garden (Tiger Balm Garden) since 2014 into Haw Par Music, a platform for cross-cultural exchange with a particular focus on music, heritage, and social programs. Although the revitalization of the building (hardware) was completed some years ago, a significant amount of the work is still on-going, and the responsibility of leading the operator's team through the revitalization process, making use of my previous experience as an architect has been beneficial. The challenge now is to oversee the operations and coordinate the programs (software) of Haw Par Music. This paper discusses the four levels of heritage conservation developed based on a unique insight on the critical role that the inter-relationship between the hardware and software plays on the success of a revitalization project.

Author Information
WU Tsan Sum Roger: rogerwu@btinternet.com

Keywords

Heritage, conservation, urban regeneration, Hong Kong, Haw Par Mansion, Haw Par Music.

1. A Brief Reflection

Heritage conservation has once again become a popular topic in Hong Kong over the past year, due to several high-profile recent events and project developments, most notably the discovery of the century-old Bishop's Hill Reservoir. Being thrust into the limelight has been the norm for heritage conservation in Hong Kong in the past two decades, with debates/discussions in the public domain making headlines many times. Although some of these debates were sometimes more emotive than rational, they nonetheless raised awareness in the community, which in turn has helped mature the city's take on the topic of heritage conservation. Despite the city's well-moulded, well-recognized image of a modern city with a rapid pace of development and change, Hong Kong also pays attention to its traditional past, and has endeavored greatly to look after its heritage assets and has come a long way in this regard. While many view the events around the demolition of Star Ferry Pier in December 2006 and Queen's Pier in February 2008 as watersheds in the city's approach to the conservation of heritage buildings, Hong Kong's efforts toward conservation had, in fact, long established roots decades earlier. The Conservancy Association was established in 1968 and has been active in the conservation of the built environment since the 1970s; the Antiquities and Monuments Ordinance (Cap. 53) was also enforced in 1976. The Antiquities Advisory Board and the Antiquities and Monuments Office were established in the same year to oversee conservation work. Notable conservation projects around that time included the preservation of the Former Kowloon-Canton Railway Clock Tower (Figure 1) in 1977.

On a personal level, despite my years of experience working on heritage buildings the world-over, the privilege of being directly involved in the revitalization project, since 2014, of the former Haw Par Mansion—a Chinese eclectic style residence built by Aw Boon Haw in 1930s—and its private garden (Tiger Balm Garden) to update it into Haw Par Music (Figure 2, page 15), a platform for cross-cultural exchange with a particular focus on music, heritage, and social programs has been tremendously rewarding and thought-provoking. Although the revitalization of the building (hardware) was completed some years ago, a significant amount of the work is still on-going, and the responsibility of leading the operator's team through the revitalization process, making use of my previous experience as an architect has been beneficial. The challenge now is in overseeing the operations and coordinating the programs (software) of Haw Par Music. This paper highlights certain details of the background of heritage conservation in Hong Kong and the inter-relationship between heritage conservation and urban regeneration in Hong Kong, as well as the four levels of heritage conservation that has been developed based on a unique insight on the critical role that the inter-relationship between the hardware and software plays on the success of a revitalization project.

2. Background of Heritage Conservation in Hong Kong

With the establishment of the Commissioner for Heritage's Office in 2008, and their "Revitalising Historic Buildings Through Partnership Scheme" (R-Scheme) and "Conserving Central" initiative, the Hong Kong Special Administrative Region government (the government) began focusing its efforts on the conservation of publicly owned (government-owned) properties. In the private sector, even though the economic argument is heavily stacked against heritage conservation because of the protection of development rights and the high land and property values in Hong Kong, over the past few years, several developers have been actively involved in high-profile

Figure 1
Former Kowloon-Canton Railway Clock Tower, Tsim Sha Tsui, Hong Kong

Figure 2
Aerial views of the former
Haw Par Mansion and Tiger
Balm Garden (left) and Haw
Par Music (right), Tai Hang,
Hong Kong

revitalization projects, such as The Mills by Nan Fung Group
(Figure 3, right), which includes a shopping belt and exhibitions,
among other innovative upgrades; State Theatre by New World
Development (Figure 4, page 16); and Central Market by Chinachem
Group (Figure 5, page 17). These are clear signs that social values—
in terms of urban regeneration—and marketing values—in terms of
branding for private sector companies involved in successful
heritage conservation projects—are beginning to be taken into
account in the development of the city of Hong Kong as a whole.

Even so, there is still much public debate on the level of success
of these private and public sector revitalization projects, with some
arguing that more should be done to protect Hong Kong's heritage,
while others say that conservation does not solve the city's more
urgent need, such as the housing problem. What is beyond dispute,
though, is the reality that accomplishing heritage conservation in
Hong Kong is extremely complex and challenging on many levels—
ownership, public engagement, planning, design implementation,
operation, management, and sustainability—and for many reasons:
high land value, unsympathetic building regulations, and lack of
opportunities to retain skills and share resources with effective
economy of scale, which is caused by the small number of such
projects. While there is a lot more to be done to make the process
more effective, it would be a grave injustice to reiterate the
difficulties without acknowledging the ground that has been covered
by many architects who have been working tirelessly in this area to
go beyond just delivering projects, to also involve raising public
awareness and engagement, as well as helping to steer professional
guidelines and government policies, namely the *Practice Guidebook
for Adaptive Re-use of and Alteration and Addition Works to Heritage
Buildings 2012* (2019 Edition).

Figure 3
Bi-city Biennale of
Urbanism\Architecture Hong
Kong 2019 (UABBHK2019) at
The Mills, Tusen Wan, Hong
Kong

15

Figure 4
Roof structure of State
Theatre (left) and the view of
the surrounding urban
environment from the rooftop
of State Theatre (right),
North Point, Hong Kong

From my experience working on several international heritage conservation projects—including King's Cross railway station (Figure 6, page 17) and Peter Jones department store (Figure 7, page 17) in London, United Kingdom, Stanislavsky Centre in Moscow, Russia (Figure 8, page 18), the British Embassy in Algiers, Algeria (Figure 9, page 18), Frank Lloyd Wright's Florida Southern College's Polk County Science Building in Florida, United States (Figure 10, page 18), and the Iron Market in Haiti (Figure 11, page 18)—I have learned that each country has its indigenous culture and sensitivities and faces its own unique set of challenges. While it is impossible to compare the success of different countries' revitalization projects and heritage conservation, even if such differences are taken into account, I believe the effort the architectural profession in Hong Kong has directed toward heritage conservation over the past decades is not insignificant. Like many other countries, there were mistakes made along the way, and there are continuing efforts taken to make sure these mistakes are not repeated. Equally, increasing effort is being made to ensure resources, techniques, and knowledge are effectively shared to better organize the solutions presented by the profession.

My involvement in the Haw Par Mansion revitalization project since its early stages, representing the non-profit organization (NPO) operating the facilities has not only provided me with a different perspective, but also helped in developing my thinking on heritage conversation further, distilling it in my mind into four distinct stages:

1. Conserve;
2. Revitalize;
3. Connect with the "spirit of the place;" and
4. Continue beyond the place.

3. The Four Levels of Heritage Conservation

3.1 Level 1: Conserve

As mentioned previously, in Hong Kong, the question "To keep or not to keep?" has often been loaded with emotive responses. This question often arises when the current use of the building has become undesirable or no longer feasible for a variety of reasons. However, the same question can also arise even when the building still serves its original use; many historic buildings need significant upgrading works to keep up with modern standards and continuously advancing technology. The history of the former Haw Par Mansion and Tiger Balm Garden, including the transfer of ownership from the Aw family to an estate developer, and the subsequent transfer after of the mansion to the government, as well as the demolition of the garden nearly twenty years ago has been detailed in the *Heritage Impact Assessment of Haw Par Mansion* and the *Revitalisation of the Haw Par Mansion Resources Kit*.[1] The resultant government ownership of the former Haw Par Mansion from these transfers meant that its preservation and conservation for the benefit of the public was secured. Even so, debates on the reasons behind, as well as the merits of various decisions made at the time of the transfer by various stakeholders still rage on today among Hong Kong's older generation who have had a first-hand experience of the mansion. However, some of the younger generation—to whom the Haw Par story is not known—might question if it is worth the effort and resources required for a conservation project of such scale.

3.2 Level 2: Revitalize

Usually, once it is decided that a heritage building is to be conserved, the next question that follows would be "What will it be

Figure 5
Central Market, Central,
Hong Kong

Figure 6
New western concourse in
front of the refurbished
Grade 1-listed historic
King's Cross railway station,
London, United Kingdom

Figure 7
Peter Jones Store, London,
United Kingdom

Figure 8
Stanislavsky Centre,
Moscow, Russia

Figure 9
British Embassy, Algiers,
Algeria

Figure 10
Polk County Science
Building, Florida Southern
College, Florida, United
States

Figure 11
Iron Market, Port-au-Prince,
Haiti

Figure 12
Main hall of Haw Par Music
showing south and north
moon gates

used for?" The revitalization of Haw Par Mansion into Haw Par Music illustrates a few interesting points on this aspect.

In 2011, Haw Par Mansion was listed as one of the Commissioner for Heritage's Office's Batch III R-Scheme candidate, for which NPOs were invited to submit applications for a renewed use of the building—either used to provide services, or for business, in the form of a social enterprise.[2] In response to the submission requirement, Haw Par Music Foundation Limited (formerly Hong Kong Music Academy) submitted detailed plans on how Haw Par Mansion and its historical significance would be preserved and interpreted, through a revitalization program, into Haw Par Music (formerly Haw Par Music Farm). They also revealed how it would be operated, so as to achieve financial viability and also provide benefits to the local community. This application submission process indicates that the selection criteria clearly identified and reflected, from the outset, the importance of the balance between respecting the building's heritage values, achieving financial sustainability, and providing social contribution as one of the key conditions for success of the adaptive reuse project—and incidentally, any of such projects, especially public sector ones.

It is also worth noting that the eligibility criteria for R-Scheme projects list that NPOs with charitable status under Section 88[3] of the Inland Revenue Ordinance (Cap. 112) are eligible to apply. This means that even if applicants have not obtained "charity" status at the time of submitting their application, they must have obtained such status within three months after the application deadline.[4] In other words, anyone with a feasible idea committed to setting up a suitable charitable organization (if not operating one already) for the running of the revitalization project is eligible to

make a submission. This reflects another key aspect for the successful delivery of adaptive reuse projects—the importance of public engagement/ownership. The fact that the R-Scheme is open to anyone with an idea (that is appropriate, feasible, has minimum impact, and most importantly, is sustainable) for a new use of a heritage building under the scheme can, in many ways, be seen as a city-wide public consultation exercise.

In late 2012, it was announced that Haw Par Music Foundation was selected as the NPO to revitalize Haw Par Mansion into Haw Par Music, in partnership with the government under their R-Scheme. After several years of planning, design development, and implementation by the design and construction teams to ensure the renovated building is fit-for-purpose as a music school, Haw Par Music officially opened its doors to public on April 1, 2019, signaling the beginning of the new chapter of the heritage building.

3.3 Level 3: Spirit of the Place

One of the often-asked questions by visitors to Haw Par Music is "Why music?" Well, there is no mystical all-encompassing one-line answer to this question that some may be expecting. So, how did the idea for a music focus come about? It happened rather organically, and once it had been identified as a feasible direction, it became a very clear vision, as music programs have, in a way, always been intrinsically connected with the place, which is made up by the "hardware" and the "software." Here, we are not merely referring to the physical space within the building that has been carefully and professionally designed so that it is fit-for-purpose, but a deeper connection with the "spirit of the place." Questions like why we have chosen to organize music programs in this place and not others, and what makes the

Figure 13
Stained glass panels on the
south moon gates in the
main hall

programs that we organize here different from those organized in other places have been, and will continue to be, asked.

A sound starting point to answer these questions is the historical background of Hong Kong around the time when the Haw Par Mansion was first constructed. Sir Cecil Clementi was the Governor of Hong Kong between 1925 and 1930, and was also the first governor who spoke Cantonese. In 1904, he even published a book titled *Cantonese Love-songs*, which translated popular Cantonese songs of that time into English. Amongst other notable achievements of Sir Clementi was his appointing Shouson Chow, a prominent Chinese merchant, as the first Chinese unofficial member of the Executive Council.

Hong Kong had long been a transient city and many at that time came to Hong Kong to look for opportunities to make a better living before returning to their homeland; Hong Kong was a stepping-stone that allowed them to hope and strive for a future elsewhere. As a result, Hong Kong thrived as a place where different cultures came together. This, coupled with the fact that Hong Kong was not burdened with the weight of hundreds of years of historical culture created plenty of opportunities for people who were free-thinking to adopt an "anything can happen" approach to life. It is within this context that Chinese eclecticism—where Chinese and Western cultures mix in art, culture, and everyday life—became the popular expressive style of the time. To some extent, this still exists strongly to this day.

In this big picture, the role of Aw Boon Haw should also be taken into account. The history of the Aw family, Haw's relationship with his brother, Aw Boon Par, the family business empire, and the buildings and gardens in Hong Kong, Singapore, and Fujian, China have been covered extensively in the text *Tiger Balm Gardens: A*

Figure 14
East and west
"flying eaves"

Chinese Billionaire's Fantasy Environments.[5] A number of key aspects of Haw's life contributed significantly to the Chinese eclecticism style used in Haw Par Mansion. The first was his exposure to, and fascination with different cultures, which he picked up during his travels for business and leisure; this, no doubt, fueled his desire to express what he had seen through his creations like the Haw Par Mansions and villas and the Tiger Balm Garden built across Hong Kong, Singapore, and Fujian, China, which reflected the variations of culture and experiences he came to be exposed to. The second was the brothers' close relationship with each other, as well as their different personalities and education background—the more outgoing Haw was sent back to Fujian for a more traditional Chinese education, while the more reserved Par remained in Yangon, Burma, and received a more "international school style" education—which encouraged the cultural exchange within the family. The final pillar was Haw's life motto: "That which is derived from society should be returned to society," which referred not only to his philanthropic endeavors, especially in education and healthcare, but also to his lifelong efforts in dissimilating to the masses the virtue of Chinese traditions and culture, as well as the views of the world gained from his privileged position as a wealthy entrepreneur, through his buildings, gardens, and newspapers, as Haw truly believed in the well-being of people through spiritual and knowledge enrichment.

The Chinese eclecticism that existed in Haw's mind allowed it to be open to an "anything is possible" (especially without the constraints of the baggage of history) mentality, which manifested perfectly in the architectural details that can still be admired in Haw Par Mansion. The two moon gates—features usually found in Chinese landscapes—are used as the mansion's main entrance doors at the front and at the garden (Figure 12, page 19); stained glass panels made in Florence, Italy that depict images of tigers and Chinese and Western birds and flora adorn the moon gates (Figure 13, page 20); two "flying eaves"—features usually found on the outside of buildings—with patterns painted on the roof tiles are the main decorative features in the main hall (Figure 14, page 20); and pictorials of the traditional Chinese folk stories *Eight Immortals Crossing the Sea* (八仙过海) (Figure 15) and *Jiang Taigong Fishing* (姜太公钓鱼) (Figure 16) adorn the underside of each "flying eave." Ms Sally Aw Sian, Haw's daughter, once related the story of how her father used to get up at 6:00 am in the morning every day to supervise the construction workers on the site during the building of Haw Par Mansion, reinforcing his almost idiosyncratic approach: beyond stylistic stereotype and any academic/theoretical research/challenge. This approach is evident, not just in the building itself, but also in the marketing and advertisements for his products, reflected by posters in Western, Chinese, and Southeast Asian styles (Figure 17, page 22).

It is against the backdrop of this history that Haw Par Music is positioned as a center for cross-cultural exchange through music, heritage, and arts, with a social initiative vein. The aim is to provide visitors opportunities to be exposed to a diversity of cultural activities and educational programs that enrich the spiritual well-being of their participants. Some programs that are good examples of how Haw Par Music reflected the "spirit of the place" include: the recording of the Italian Opera RITA by Gaetano Donizetti in the main hall (later aired on Hong Kong television)(Figure 18, page 22); two unannounced open rehearsal sessions that took place in the main hall, alongside a Cantonese opera exhibition in the adjacent former dining room; a performance by Contempo Lion Dance, the "Best

Figure 15
Eight Immortals Crossing the Sea pictorial on the underside of the main hall's east-side "flying eave"

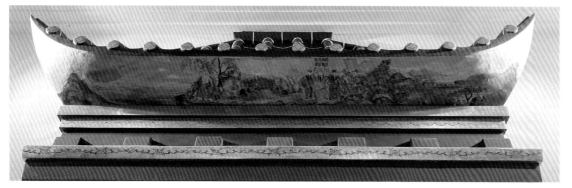

Figure 16
Jiang Taigong Fishing pictorial on the underside of the main hall's west-side "flying eave"

Figure 17
The different styles of Tiger Balm's marketing posters: Chinese style (left), Western style (middle), and Southeast Asian style (right)

Special Venue Performance" category winner in the 2020 Hong Kong Dance Award, and whose repertoire updates the traditional lion dance artform with a combination of parkour, contemporary Chinese dance, flamenco, and Nanyin (a traditional type of Cantonese opera that is popular in Southern China; it is a musical performing art central to the culture of the people of Minnan in southern Fujian Province along China's southeastern coast, and to Minnan populations overseas), which delivered an immersive and captivating Haw-style eclecticism that aptly commemorated the blend of the different style of aesthetics and architecture in the venue (Figure 19, page 23); an inter-generational orchestra performance that combined musicians of different ages, skill levels, and nationality (Figure 20, page 23); the project with the Hong Kong Society for the Blind, in which the key component was an inclusive learning and sharing of sensory experiences between fully sighted and visually impaired visitors (Figure 21, page 23); and an event that celebrated the thirtieth anniversary of the Visegrad Group (V4) with an exhibition of the winning entries of a poster competition; it was a performance that included contemporary and classical music from all four countries of the group and a folk dance number from the V4 region performed by a local dance group (Figure 22, page 24).

It should be mentioned that the Contempo Lion Dance performance and the project with the Hong Kong Society for the Blind would not have been possible without the involvement of the architects who undertook the revitalization project, in that their efforts went beyond their call of duty to deliver a fit-for-purpose project that was able to support the hosting of these events. They demonstrated their commitment to the project, instead of treating it merely as a commission, with their continued involvement, understanding, and appreciation of the "spirit of the place"—the Haw Par ethos.

Figure 18
The recording of the Italian Opera *RITA* by Gaetano Donizetti in the main hall of Haw Par Music

3.4 Level 4: Beyond the Place

With great challenge, and perhaps with some contradiction, the highest level that conservation projects should aim toward is to take the "spirit of the place" beyond the place. Haw Par Music has taken small steps toward achieving this goal through outreach programs in which faculties and students perform in other locations to promote programs that ring home the Haw Par ethos (Figure 23, page 24). This paves the way to establish similar programs, like those organized at Haw Par Music—with the same Haw Par ethos—in other locations, therefore taking the spirit beyond the place, and through that, echoing the way of the Aw family—after building Haw Par Mansion and Tiger Balm Garden in Hong Kong, they built other similar mansions, villas, and gardens in Singapore and Fujian.

In the long term, and looking at the bigger picture, when combined with other conservation projects that take the idea of the "spirit of the place" forward in the same way that the Haw Par ethos— built on roots that are reflective of Hong Kong's cultural history and identity then and now—does, can their collective spirit metamorphize to become more reflective of the "spirit of Hong Kong?"

4. Epilogue: Can the Profession Do More?

Among the many skills that architects possess, the ability to consider various contextual, planning, environmental, design, and technical aspects of any project before making decisions on the suitable way forward can be considered the skill that stands out the most. For conservation projects to successfully achieve the four levels of heritage conservation discussed, there is a need to take

Figure 19
A performance by Contempo Lion Dance (directed by Daniel Yeung), the "Best Special Venue Performance" category winner in the 2020 Hong Kong Dance Award, held in the study area of Haw Par Music

Figure 20
Inter-generational orchestra performance at the rooftop Function Suite

Figure 21
Joint project with the Hong Kong Society for the Blind

23

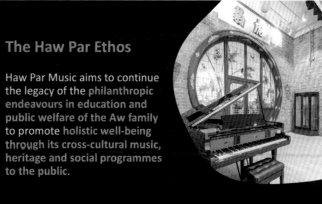

Figure 22
Folk dance performance in
the Visegrad Group 30th
Anniversary event held in
Haw Par Music

Figure 23
Haw Par Ethos

this skill even further, to consider beyond merely physical functions, to the more philosophical concept that is the "spirit of the place," right from the beginning of the project.

There is a need to engage the client/operator further to avoid the disconnect that often occurs post-construction by connecting with operational issues beyond the completion of construction stages. On the client engagement front, post-contract processes need to be developed beyond the client-and-consultant relationship. Better still if architects can step out of the role of consultants and offer their skill sets and services as initiators, drivers, champions, and facilitators for these projects.

Notes

1. Centre for Architectural Heritage Research, *Heritage Impact Assessment of Haw Par Mansion* (Hong Kong: Antiquities and Monuments Office, 2014), https://www.amo.gov.hk/form/HIA_Report_HPM.pdf; The Commissioner for Heritage's Office, *Revitalisation of the Haw Par Mansion Resources Kit* (Hong Kong: The Commissioner for Heritages' Office, 2011), https://www.heritage.gov.hk/en/doc/rhbtp/Haw_Par_Mansion_Resource_Kit_eng.pdf.
2. "Revitalising Historic Buildings Through Partnership Scheme," About the Scheme page, The Commissioner for Heritage's Office website, https://www.heritage.gov.hk/en/rhbtp/about.htm.
3. Section 88 provides that a charity is exempt from profits tax subject to the fulfillment of certain conditions in relation to the trade or business carried on by the charity concerned.
4. "Revitalising Historic Buildings Through Partnership Scheme," About the Scheme page, The Commissioner for Heritage's Office website, https://www.heritage.gov.hk/en/rhbtp/about.htm.
5. Judith Brandel and Tina Turbeville, *Tiger Balm Gardens: A Chinese Billionaire's Fantasy Environments* (Hong Kong: The Aw Boon Haw Foundation, 1998).

Reference

Zheng, V. *The Haw Par Family: An Exploration of Its Rise and Fall.* Hong Kong: Chung Hwa Book Company, 2018.

Figure Credits

Figure 1: Former Kowloon-Canton Railway Clock Tower, Tsim Sha Tsui, Hong Kong (Hong Kong Antiquities and Monuments Office, https://www.amo.gov.hk).
Figure 2: Aerial views of the former Haw Par Mansion and Tiger Balm Garden (left) and Haw Par Music (right), Tai Hang, Hong Kong (courtesy of Haw Par Music Foundation Limited, Hong Kong).
Figure 3: Bi-city Biennale of Urbanism\Architecture Hong Kong 2019 (UABBHK2019) at The Mills, Tusen Wan, Hong Kong (courtesy of The Hong Kong Institute of Architects Biennale Foundation).
Figure 4: Roof structure of State Theatre (left) and the view of the surrounding urban environment from the rooftop of State Theatre (right), North Point, Hong Kong (author's photo).
Figure 5: Central Market, Central, Hong Kong (Candice Chau, "Hong Kong's Central Market Comes Back to Life but Conservationist Takes Issue with 'Gentrification'," *Hong Kong Free Press*, August 26, 2021, https://hongkongfp.com/2021/08/26/hong-kongs-central-market-comes-back-to-life-but-conservationist-takes-issue-with-gentrification/).
Figure 6: New western concourse in front of the refurbished Grade 1-listed historic King's Cross railway station, London, United Kingdom (author's photo).
Figure 7: Peter Jones Store, London, United Kingdom (courtesy of John McAslan + Partners, London, United Kingdom).
Figure 8: Stanislavsky Centre, Moscow, Russia (courtesy of John McAslan + Partners, London, United Kingdom).
Figure 9: British Embassy, Algiers, Algeria (courtesy of John McAslan + Partners, London, United Kingdom).
Figure 10: Polk County Science Building, Florida Southern College, Florida, United States (courtesy of John McAslan + Partners, London, United Kingdom).
Figure 11: Iron Market, Port-au-Prince, Haiti (courtesy of John McAslan + Partners, London, United Kingdom).
Figure 12: Main hall of Haw Par Music showing south and north moon gates (courtesy of Haw Par Music Foundation, Hong Kong).
Figure 13: Stained glass panels on the south moon gates in the main hall (author's photo).
Figure 14: East and west "flying eaves" in the main hall of Haw Par Music (author's photo).
Figure 15: *Eight Immortals Crossing the Sea* pictorial on the underside of the main hall's east-side "flying eave" (author's photo).
Figure 16: *Jiang Taigong Fishing* pictorial on the underside of the main hall's west-side "flying eave" (author's photo).
Figure 17: The different styles of Tiger Balm's marketing posters: Chinese style (left), Western style (middle) and Southeast Asian style (right) (Aw Family Collection, Hong Kong).
Figure 18: The recording of the Italian Opera RITA by Gaetano Donizetti in the main hall of Haw Par Music (photo by Berton Chang; image courtesy of Let Me Plan It Co.).
Figure 19: A performance by Contempo Lion Dance (directed by Daniel Yeung), the "Best Special Venue Performance" category winner in the 2020 Hong Kong Dance Award, held in the study area of Haw Par Music (image courtesy of Hong Kong Arts Development Council and The Hong Kong Jockey Club Charities Trust).
Figure 20: Inter-generational orchestra performance at the rooftop Function Suite (courtesy of Haw Par Music Foundation, Hong Kong).
Figure 21: Joint project with the Hong Kong Society for the Blind (courtesy of Hong Kong Society for the Blind).
Figure 22: Folk dance performance in the Visegrad Group 30th Anniversary event held in Haw Par Music (courtesy of The Consulate General of the Republic of Poland in Hong Kong).
Figure 23: Haw Par Ethos (courtesy of Haw Par Music Foundation, Hong Kong).

Optimized Strategies Concerning Sharing and Regeneration of Heritage Spaces in Old Urban Quarters

Taking the Historical Urban Area in Yingping District, Xiamen, as an Example

WANG Shao Sen, Professor, Class 1 Registered Architect, School of Architecture and Civil Engineering, Xiamen University, China

ZHANG Ke Han, Doctoral Candidate, School of Architecture and Civil Engineering, Xiamen University, China

ZHAO Long, Doctoral Candidate, School of Architecture and Civil Engineering, Xiamen University, China

QUE Quan Hong, Doctoral Candidate, School of Architecture and Civil Engineering, Xiamen University, China

Author Information

WANG Shao Sen: ymcai@xmu.edu.cn

ZHANG Ke Han: kehan_zhang_design@163.com

ZHAO Long: amoyheritage@stu.xmu.edu.cn

QUE Quan Hong: 364761621@qq.com

Abstract

Stock planning and heritage regeneration are two themes that are usually broached in the conservation of historic spaces in old urban quarters in Xiamen, China. In the conditions of a low quality of living, environmental pollution, transportation congestion, and disordered management, the old districts in the city are facing big challenges. The main aim of this study is to develop a strategy to share and regenerate the urban space in old urban quarters and activate vitality in districts by providing and sharing new spaces and protecting the local historical culture and infrastructure for both residents and tourists. Through the introduction of optimized strategies, there can be new possibilities for the old urban quarter of Yingping District to create: a livable space with multilevel people, a public space with high-quality shared infrastructure, and a cultural space with historical characteristic. By analyzing the condition of this area, new solutions can be applied, which include the conservation of historical buildings, social structure adjustment, façade renewal, transportation reorganization, art activation, and infrastructure development. This study provides a reference for the practice of sharing and renewal of the built heritage in historic urban areas.

Keywords

Historic urban area, sharing and regeneration, heritage space, old urban quarters, Yingping District.

a. Datong Road in the early 1930s   b. Datong Road in the late 1930s   c. Datong Road in 1938

d. Datong Road in 1940   e. Datong Road in 1950   f. Datong Road in 1980

Figure 1
Historical images of Datong
Road, from 1930 to 1980

1. Introduction

Often, old urban quarters in Asia are always associated with the people's collective memory of the past, their sense of place and time, and local and community identity. It also generates an intangible value created by sharing an area's regional characteristics and uniqueness, which constructs the spirit of the urban space. However, next to the advancement of local urbanization, urban development, and drastic changes in social, economic, political, and cultural conditions, the built environment of old quarters has fallen into a kind of incompatibility with the new needs of users because of the degradation of neighborhood service functions (resulting in low living quality and disordered management), harsh environment (for example, environment pollution), and low space-bearing capacity (such as transportation congestion and high population density).[1,2] Because of these unpleasant conditions, community residents and activities have gradually moved away from old urban quarters, and aging, population migration, and declining livability, vitality, and sustainability have become the main characteristics of these areas.

Both in theory and in practice, the cultural enhancement, economic stimulation, space regeneration, and sharing of old urban quarters in the conservation process are unavoidable tasks when wanting to stimulate these approaches' strong potential and spill-over benefits.

This study focuses on sharing and regeneration-led optimized strategies for the heritage space in the old urban quarter in Yingping District, Xiamen, and discusses the revitalization of this heritage space along the following strategies:

1. Adaptive recycle framework for regeneration;
2. Hybridizing culture, economies, and creative processes;
3. Reshaping the rich life experience of human habitation; and
4. Empowerment of the social and cultural values that are locally embedded, to achieve goals of sustainability in old urban quarters in the new scenario of stock planning in China's planning practice.

2. Background

2.1 The Study Area: The Old Yingping District Along Xiamen Harbor
The Xiamen harbor area, which includes the old Yingping District, was an offshoot from southwest old Xiamen City located in the south of Xiamen Island, and it expanded along the coastline from north to south, with shops and stores opened by local people and fishermen. The selected research site is situated in southeast Yingping District—which covers an area of about 25 hectares—and extends to Kaiyuan Road in the north and Datong Road in the south; the east boundary is formed by Erwang Street and Guangcai Street, which is a small alley, and the western boundary is marked by Dayuan Road, which is a famous restaurant street in the district. The whole area spans about 3.5 hectares and includes nine main alleys, which are about 3 to 5 meters wide, and more than ten narrow secondary alleys, which are so narrow they only allow a person or two to pass at any one time.

The buildings along the main roads, Kaiyuan Road and Datong Road, are shophouses in typical Xiamen Decoration style and most of them have maintained their historical characteristics. Many of the buildings have been restored over the past five years. There are also more than ten historic and heritage buildings located in this area. Most of them feature the typical Xiamen Decoration style, while some display the Nanyang and Minnan style. The local government attaches high importance to these buildings and almost all of them have come to become protected buildings, or are registered to be protected.

Figure 2
Yingping District, 2021

For example, the former Xiamen Federation of Trade Unions building is protected by the government as a "Provincial Cultural Heritage Site" and the old Datong Road committee building and the Old Street Museum are conserved as "Significant Protected Historic Buildings." Most of these heritage and historic buildings are well preserved and attract many citizens and tourists, especially Old Theatre Plaza, a square surrounded by other heritage buildings, located in the west sector of this area; it was named so because of a dismantled old theater nearby. This square was restored five years ago with a new space organization and updated facilities. The nice environment and new public spaces make it a key public center for the whole district and every Saturday, the local community organizes performances and exhibitions in this square. The themes of these shows and exhibitions are usually registered on the "World Non-material Cultural Heritage List," and such shows serve to highly increase the culture and living quality of Yingping District.

2.2 Current Issues and Challenges Faced

The team's research on Yingping District, as well as casual chats with the local people highlight some key issues:

1. Chaos in traffic flow—the high density of buildings inside the selected study area has created insufficient walking space for pedestrians. The traffic capacity is also often seriously reduced due to the lack of standards in reasonable urban public transport planning, as well as traffic chaos and congestion caused by the narrow streets and dense population.

2. The deterioration of the buildings and the lack of repair has directly resulted in the decline of the service function of the old urban quarter—many of the buildings were built illegally and in a haphazard fashion, resulting in complicated building conditions.

Moreover, the "messy" and unclear ownership background of the houses in this area often generate disputes over property rights, which have made neighborhood renewal difficult. There needs to be a strategic implementation and use of institutional design and district renewal.

3. Much of the infrastructure is old and creaky, such as the cables and pipes, and are in a disordered "rough, unfinished" state as proper engineering design to conceal service and mechanical functions was not carried out. This highly affects the overall historical environment.

4. Because of the extensive land use through history, the density and capacity of the old quarter have become too high, and the residents'/renters' living quality has become incompatible with space demands, and not been essentially improved. Many of the buildings are connected, creating plenty of "dark areas" that get no natural sunlight all year round. Adding to that, public spaces and activity areas can also be rarely found in this urban village, and there is also a lack of green spaces.

5. Commercial activities in Yingping District, especially along Datong Road and Kaiyuan Road keep slowing down, thereby causing weakness in the area's commercial vitality—with the number of tourists decreasing yearly, a serious decline in commercial and business opportunities has resulted, which has given rise to an appreciable impact on the commercial and tourism condition of Yingping District. One of the urgent solutions required in Yingping District is a feasible and successful way to attract commercial businesses and tourists back to the area through planning tools.

6. The utilization of culture and heritage is not sufficient— the previous conservation and regeneration strategy for Xiamen old quarter was conservative, and remains so.

27

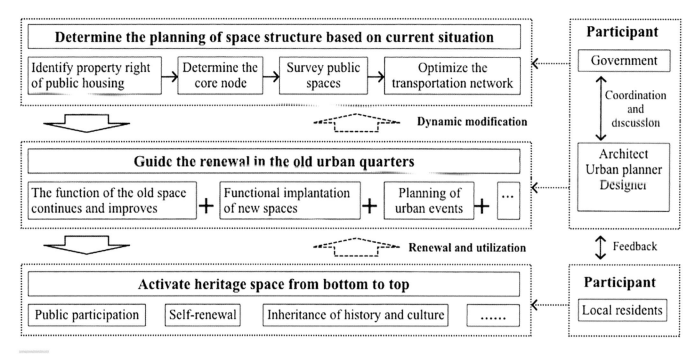

Figure 3
Recycle framework for
regeneration

The strategy focused on protection, instead of management and utilization. Although some cultural activities have been held around the Old Theatre Plaza, the cultural atmosphere hardly extends to other places. The investigation and utilization of local allusions, folk religion, living customs, and commercial history need to be improved.

Based on these overall analyses of Yingping District, optimized strategies for sharing and regeneration of its heritage space, along with design approaches, need to be developed to allow Yingping District to build a hierarchical living historic quarter, as well as create a vibrant quarter and a cultural quarter with collective memories and feelings.

3. Sharing and Regeneration-led Optimized Strategies for Heritage Spaces in Old Urban Quarters

3.1 Designing an Adaptive Recycle Framework for Regeneration

The current heritage space in Yingping District faces prominent problems, such as complicated building property rights, population loss, and a general indifference toward local culture. Relying solely on the government or design teams to update and revitalize the area would not be an effective way to solve these problems. To this end, this paper designs an adaptive recycle framework for regeneration that can guide the renewal and revitalization of heritage spaces in old urban quarters (Figure 3), and also the heritage space in Yingping District.

The first stage in this framework is fundamental, which is to determine the planning of space structure based on the current situation. It needs to be done by the government, together with a team of architects, urban planners, and designers. With the help of government departments, the construction team can receive full disclosure on the ownership rights of buildings in heritage spaces in old urban quarters. A review of property rights can then enable the team to ascertain the distribution of public and private housing/buildings and mixed public and private housing; public housing usually make up a smaller number and are more scattered, and they are also more likely to be renewed, which can be carried out without obstructions. With regards to private housing and mixed public and private housing, it is necessary to fully communicate with residents and be transparent on the renewal direction planned for the whole area. Second, the core nodes of heritage spaces in old urban quarters should be identified, as shown in Figure 4 (page 29), which reflects the selected study area in Yingping District. Through the identification of core nodes, the vitality of spaces can be activated on a "priority" basis to pave the way for guiding private housing toward self-renewal. Picking out public spaces within the site is another essential part of the process as the construction team needs to integrate existing plazas and parklands in the regeneration to provide open spaces for residents and visitors.

Finally, it is also necessary to clarify the main roadways, secondary roadways, main roads, and secondary roads in old urban quarters. Through the cascading of street spaces, the composite use of functions can be promoted. Upon the systematic collation of these aspects, it can then be possible to gain a deeper understanding of heritage space structures, as well an old urban quarter's potential for renewal and revitalization, which is a prerequisite for the next phase of spatial conservation and utilization.

The second stage in the revitalization needs to be completed by both government departments and the construction team. The physical space that has been identified in the first stage can be revitalized in two main ways, depending on the usage needs of the different groups of people, for example, residents and tourists.

The first would be to continue and improve the function of the old space. It is necessary for old spaces to be preserved with the potential for renewal, while continuing the original function of the corresponding buildings. Such initiatives ensure that heritage spaces in old urban quarters are maintained with maximum authenticity and integrity, without overly destroying the purest spatial relationships of the streets and alleys. The second way would be to facilitate the functional implantation of new spaces. For part of the rebuilt or inventory space, new functions should be introduced. These new functions can change the industrial structure of heritage spaces in old urban quarters and attract more young people to move in. Further, new urban events should be created based on the space's unique local history, culture, and living environment. The second stage plays a connecting role in the whole process of heritage space renewal. Over time, this will also have an impact on the spatial planning structure defined in the first phase in the concrete implementation process, which in turn will lead to dynamic adjustments.

The third stage is a bottom-up process, in which residents activate the spaces. Through preliminary popularization work with residents, a form of revitalization is introduced, though not directly. During this preliminary popularization, it is necessary, and benefitting, to actively spread and promote the area's local culture, and to raise the residents' awareness of conservation and their sense of identity through extensive publicity, to ultimately result in autonomous public participation.

In this third stage, it is predicted that residents will start to renew/revitalize their houses (forming the "private housing" section) on their own. With their understanding of history and culture, residents can—through refurbishing their private homes— update the heritage space to maintain its efficiency and frequency of use. A bottom-up approach ensures that the entire process of renewing and revitalizing the heritage space is dynamic and recycled.

In summary, this framework can fully integrate people, architecture, and local culture closely to truly revive heritage spaces in old urban quarters.

3.2 Hybridizing Culture, Economies, and Creative Processes with the Heritage Space in Yingping District for Sharing

Cultural heritage can indeed inspire local creativity, which can, in turn, have a positive impact on economic development through the generation of new and original ideas.[3, 4] In the old historic urban quarter of Yingping District, the key points are people, culture, economy, and the area's heritage. The revival of this area includes improvements like increasing the people's living quality, the utilization and value presentation of the heritage of the area, and introducing a characteristic commercial mode. Based on the review and analysis of Yingping District, a planning and design strategy that follows the recycle framework above is suggested. The strategy creates a planning and space structure that promotes "one axis with two double areas, three centers, two belts, and multiple nodes" arrangement within the selected study area, as described in Figure 5 (page 30). Such a planning approach focuses on making full use of the heritage and culture of Yingping District and creates a sharing and active heritage space to improve living quality and the area's tourism value.

Figure 4
Heritage space and buildings within the selected research area in Yingping District

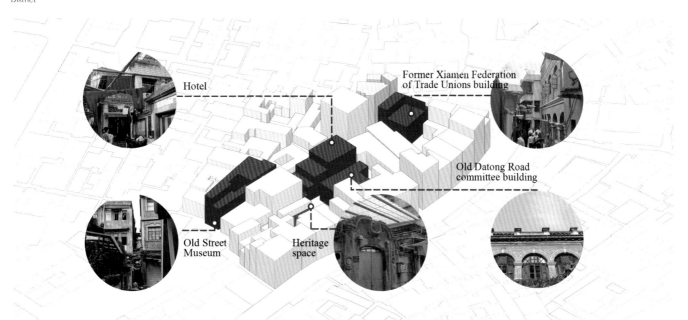

Hotel

Former Xiamen Federation of Trade Unions building

Old Datong Road committee building

Old Street Museum

Heritage space

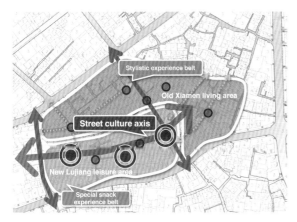

Figure 5
Planning strategy for the
selected study area in
Yingping District adapted to
the recycle framework for
regeneration

It is possible to generate a historical route by renewing selected historical buildings and spaces. The process is described in Figure 6 (below), and starts with determining the rightful owner/s of the buildings in order to ascertain which can be reconstructed or dismantled.

The next step would be to identify appropriate historical zones, like Old Theatre Plaza, the former Xiamen Federation of Trade Unions building, and Haoyue Temple. Most of these buildings are publicly owned, which provides leeway for the government to reconstruct them. By renewing these key buildings and spaces, they can guide and encourage/motivate other privately owned buildings to be reconstructed. Dismantling specific buildings in this area can also generate new public spaces to create more open and green spaces, which can improve the living quality within this area.

By comprehensively optimizing the environmental quality, stimulating the vitality of the space, and promoting the overall improvement of the economic and social value of Yingping District's old urban quarter, new ways of living can be established to form a new historical quarter.

Another way would be to promote a social population guidance strategy. This entails first adjusting the industrial structure, which includes the reinforcement of tertiary industries to optimize the population structure to attract well-educated people to join the community. The second step is the optimization of management. By improving infrastructure and the appropriate management of buildings, the population mobility can be controlled to maintain the stability of the population structure. The third step would be for the government to draw up more policies focused on settlement and education to support non-natives that are well educated, so as to nurture a population structure that is highly educated and skilled. Fourth is the protection of local people and culture,

Figure 6
The process of planning an
intervention for the sharing
and regeneration of a
heritage space in an old
urban quarter

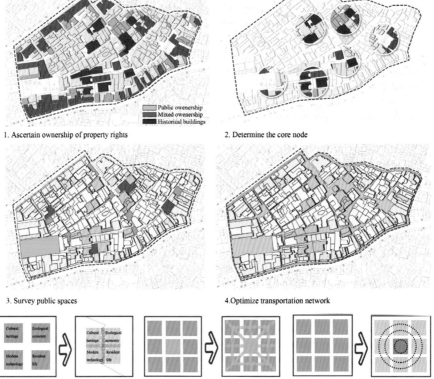

1. Ascertain ownership of property rights

Public ownership
Mixed ownership
Historical buildings

2. Determine the core node

3. Survey public spaces

4. Optimize transportation network

Functonal complex utilization   Create public spaces   Awaken street vitality with nodes

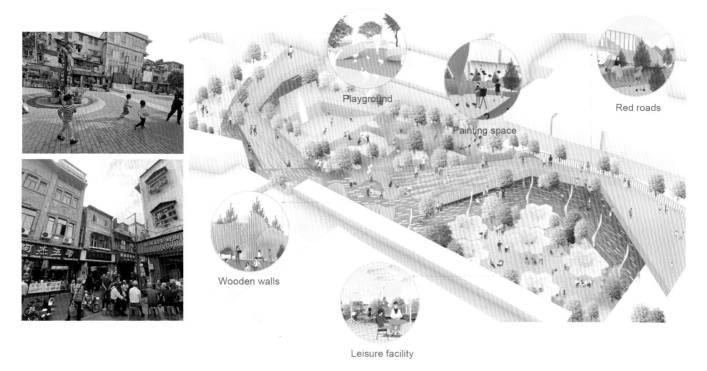

Playground

Painting space

Red roads

Wooden walls

Leisure facility

Figure 7
Optimized strategy for
reshaping the rich
experience in Old Theatre
Plaza

especially those who possess traditional skills, such as Minnan storytellers and Gezai opera performers. This will help maintain the diversity of the population and bring vitality to the community.

3.3 Reshaping the Rich Life Experience of Human Habitation

Attractive local culture, elegant historical and stylistic buildings, and fascinating performances and exhibitions can be considered the key points of creating sharing public spaces. Take the Old Theatre Plaza as an example; the natives shared that the square is a leisure space for locals, which attracts people to stay, but they do not feel enough culture in the space. Taking this issue into consideration, a design is proposed, as shown in Figure 7 (above). Two bridges are designed to connect the square and two historic buildings, one of them being the Old Street Museum, with signages designed to show local allusions and folk religion.

The bridges create more spaces that have different characteristics, especially shading spaces that consist of facilities with different functions, such as increased seating, fitness facilities, and a playground. A fountain is designed between the bridges and this promenade area can double as an outdoor cinema in the evenings by setting up a screen and projector. Guiding signages can be redesigned to attract tourists to visit the museum and the many famous shops located close by. Designing places in this way can centralize the advantages of a big area like this, which consists of historic buildings, public spaces, and people, and create a regional center that attracts more people to visit.

Another solution would be to utilize historical buildings. One aspect of this would be to control the buildings' style—the reconstruction of old buildings and the construction of new buildings should maintain a uniform native architectural style, like

Xiamen Decoration style or Minnan style. Another aspect would be material control to encourage the use of traditional materials like Minnan red bricks.

For example, a new design may be employed to improve the living quality in Meditation Street, a narrow ally in the north part of the selected study area (Figure 8, page 32). This proposed solution selects an area around a historical building that is in good condition, and which has stylistic value. Other old public buildings around the area are dismantled to open the area, and in their place, a teahouse, a platform, and a coffee shop are built, beside the historical building, to generate more possibilities for activity and provide more public and green spaces.

3.4 Empowerment of the Social and Cultural Values That are Locally Embedded

The heritage space in the old urban quarter in Yingping District is rich in historical and cultural resources. These cultures have a very important role in enhancing the local economic and social values. In theory, and practice, to make Yingping District a cultural quarter that invokes strong associated feelings among the people, it is necessary to adapt its revitalization to the local fabric and organically integrate multiple cultures into the design.

First, an in-depth cataloging of local culture should be conducted. The Yingping District contains a variety of cultures such as screen culture, Chinese revolution culture, Minnan culture, Nanyang culture, and commercial culture. Different cultural values should be distinguished and identified, and the most significant cultural features should be highlighted.

To guarantee the effective implementation of the plan, one of the most central steps is to comply with public policy and master planning directives set by the government. According to the protection requirements proposed in the *Xiamen Zhongshan Road Historic and Cultural Quarter Protection Planning* document, there are four main methods for the development and utilization of tangible cultural heritage spaces in an old urban quarter.

1. The first method is to use it as is. In this method, the historic space is required to continue to maintain its original function and use; this may include various types of religious buildings and residential houses.

2. The second method is the "historical display" approach. Combined with its historical function, the heritage space will also serve as a historical and cultural display site open to the public, forming a thematic pavilion.

3. Third on the list is to design the heritage space into a cultural activity place. Combining historical resources and environmental conditions, the heritage space can be used as a place for public activities that showcase culture and art—such as museums.

4. The last method is to develop a heritage space as a tourism service. Based on the cultural characteristics of the heritage space, it can serve as a commercial place to serve the community and support tourism—such as B&B hotels, cafés, and casual dining restaurants/bars, which are all important spaces for foreign visitors and tourists to experience local culture.

When applying the four provisions in the *Xiamen Zhongshan Road Historic and Cultural Quarter Protection Planning* document to the paper's selected study area in Yingping District, the following suggestions are made to better guide cultural inheritance.

Haoyue Temple, which is locally the most religious and cultural building in the district is preserved as it is, so that it can continue to perform its daily religious rituals and maintain its religious function. The temple will also be extended at the back by adding a leisure landscape pavilion which can be used as a good place for

residents to catch up on what's happening in the neighborhood and exchange some chit-chat (Figure 9, below). By preserving the function of Haoyue Temple as it is, the local customs and culture will not be destroyed, and the lifestyle of the residents can be accommodated to the greatest extent.

Red Street, a historical street with ties to the Chinese revolution culture, has many available architectural nodes, and will be updated in a completely different way from Haoyue Temple. The former Xiamen Federation of Trade Unions building is located at the entrance of Red Street, and it would be ideal to utilize the second method to make it into an exhibition hall to showcase Xiamen's revolution history. The third method is best applied to the historic building opposite the old Datong Road committee building to make it into a storytelling house that reflects the traditional cultural characteristics of Red Street. The original unused buildings around the area will also be replaced in accordance with the fourth method, to be transformed into bookstores and coffee shops to attract more young people to Red Street (Figure 10, page 33). Finally, the scattered cultural resources are strung together into a network. Two important routes are planned in the regeneration design of Yingping District. One of them is the Citizen Life Route (Figure 11a, page 33), which links places with local life, such as Haoyue Temple, traditional Chinese catering, and a teahouse. The other route is the Cultural Experience Route (Figure 11b, page 33). This route relies mainly on local culture and uses historical buildings and cultural spaces for focused renewal to form tourism nodes with special features, such as the Old Street Museum and the former Xiamen Federation of Trade Unions building. Both routes can fully demonstrate to the public the vitality and future plasticity of the heritage space in Yingping District. A network of heritage spaces in the old urban quarter can be formed to achieve true sustainability.

Figure 8
Unitilization of historical buildings in Meditation Street

Teahouse at the entrance of the street   Platform for recreation   Coffee shop

Figure 9
Planning and design for Haoyue Temple

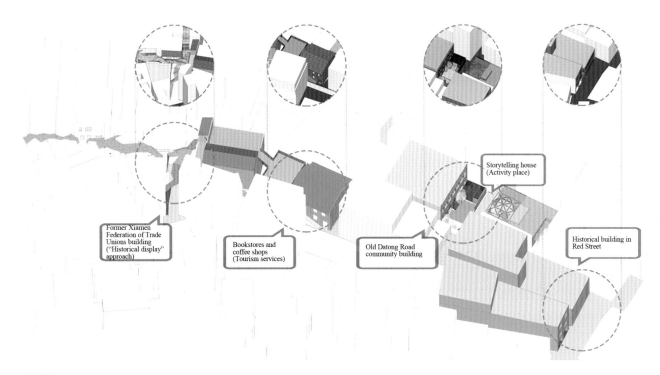

Figure 10
Core space design of Red Street

Labels in figure:
- Former Xiamen Federation of Trade Unions building ("Historical display" approach)
- Bookstores and coffee shops (Tourism services)
- Old Datong Road community building
- Storytelling house (Activity place)
- Historical building in Red Street

Figure 11
Planning of Citizen Life Route (top) and Cultural Experience Route (bottom)

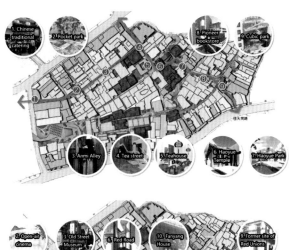

4. Discussion

People, buildings, and local culture are the key elements of sharing and regeneration-led optimized strategies to preserve culture, an area's history, and its heritage spaces. The analysis and application of the strategies proposed for Yingping District reveal that, if employed correctly, these strategies can facilitate the sustainability of its old urban quarter (as well as other old quarters in other areas) within conservation and development agendas drafted by the city. From an academic perspective, the nature of sustainability incorporates social, cultural, and economic dimensions, as well as demonstrates strong interdependencies between environment and people.[5, 6] The sustainability of old urban quarters is reflected, first, in the condition of their physical capital, which is represented by their physical configuration—such as geographical feature, urban infrastructure, old buildings, landmark, the various community/landscape layers (architectural, cultural, and historical fabrics, and so on), morphology, vegetation, and townscape. The second contingent of sustainability is the socio-cultural values implied by the first group of factors and the roles that these values perform in defining cultural diversity, sense of place, sense of history, the place's spirit, community belonging, business patterns, and social cohesion. Cultural aspects that exist with local society, and which are enriched by the built environment can be an adequate tool for expressing history, the spirit of a place, urban image, and imagination, and even predict the future.

Two other significant concepts are also usually incorporated into the design plan of sharing and regeneration, which are the Historic Urban Landscape Approach and the People-centered Approach. Applied to this research's selected study

33

area in Yingping District, the two concepts aim to re-establish the connection between the management of the old urban quarter, contemporary urban development, and the regional, geological, and historical, context.

According to the Historic Urban Landscape Approach by UNESCO, in order to pursue sustainable development in old urban quarters, the steps should respect local communities in their quest for development and adaptation, while retaining the characteristics and values linked to the community's and quarter's history, collective memory, and heritage environment.[7] In the People-centered Approach, cultural heritage in old urban quarters is viewed as having been created by people, where it is created for the people.[8] Understandably, human activities occur in every component of cultural heritage, as viewed in accordance with this approach, which affects urban and social growth—such as the social class—economy, religion, politics, belief, and technology, which has an influence on the built environment on various levels. Taking a people-centered approach in townscape studies is not merely a suggestion for increasing participation within a management system, but it also addresses a core component of heritage management—the people who are connected to this heritage—and ensures that they are included as an integral element of conserving that heritage. The People-centered Approach retains focus along a more qualitative and humanistic spectrum. Here, the role of ethnic culture and urban characteristics is highlighted, and the urban image, and images, are improved.

5. Conclusion

This study discusses a light intervention and operability in the sharing and regeneration of old urban quarters, and focuses on system regeneration/system establishment, structural adjustment, relationship building, space connection, and artistic intervention. It is committed to building a hierarchical living historic quarter, and to create a quality vibrant quarter and a cultural quarter with both collective memories and feelings. In general, this study improves the life experience of community residents and meets the different needs of locals and tourists. The solutions proposed promote the improvement of old urban quarters to boost vitality, and advocate the continuation and maintenance of urban texture and characteristics, and local spirit.

Transformations within old urban quarters, in the context of current society—even when issues concerning the historic environment are in question—is not impossible. The transformation of the different components in old urban quarters illustrates the new tendency of local society; perhaps some changes were impossible in the past, but it doesn't mean that the component cannot be changed in the future. Therefore, the relationship of the modern society and old urban quarters is experienced rapidly, and transforms by evolving within this cycle—or more precisely—within a dynamic world.

Nevertheless, the transformation will be a stable equilibrium and continue changing only when new strategies are fostered, that are capable of matching new situations based on a reasonable planning process. The paradoxical roles of transformation are illustrated in the evident impact of the old urban quarter in Yingping District—in how transformation brings about changes within such an environment to generate new characteristics, yet also evokes feelings and memories relevant to its history.

Given that such changing variables of old urban quarters are emplaced within the framework of conservation and development, this paper aids to deepen the understanding of sharing and regeneration, sustainability, townscapes, urban morphology, and their relation to practical situations.

The local culture with hybrid characteristics is generated as a stable variable in the historic environment. Changing variables exert multiple effects on old urban quarters, like in the subsequent use of old buildings to promote heritage tourism in the heritage space as an innovative means to foster economic and social benefits for the community. Transformation brings about new forms of social life, concepts, and attitude toward old urban quarters. It produces a new sensorial dimension with profound effects. The activities related to transformation have created a powerful impact on all aspects within old urban quarters, ranging from the economy of the heritage site, the livelihood of the inhabitants, and urban development strategies, to more critical interrogations of changing urban identities under neoliberal globalization. This, in turn, facilitates a new interpretation of old urban quarters and a new image that redefines the identity and spirit of a place within the practical value of optimized strategies.

Acknowledgments

This paper was fully supported by a grant (51878581) from the National Natural Science Foundation of China. The authors would like to thank all the referees for their valuable comments.
The authors are also especially indebted to An Hong Jie, Liu Yang, Li Xi Da, and Wu Yun Jie for their assistance in the research and planning of this paper.

Notes
1. Naciye Doratli, "Revitalizing Historic Urban Quarters: A Model for Determining the Most Relevant Strategic Approach," *European Planning Studies* 13, no. 5 (2005): 749–772.
2. Rokhsaneh Rahbarianyazd, "Sustainability in Historic Urban Environments: Effect of Gentrification in the Process of Sustainable Urban Revitalization," *Journal of Contemporary Urban Affairs* 1, no. 1 (2017): 1–9.
3. Silvia Cerisola, "A New Perspective on the Cultural Heritage–Development Nexus: The Role of Creativity," *Journal of Cultural Economics* 43, no. 1 (2019): 21–56.
4. Roberta Capello, Silvia Cerisola, and Giovanni Perucca, "Cultural Heritage, Creativity, and Local Development: A Scientific Research Program," *Regeneration of the Built Environment from a Circular Economy Perspective* (2020): 11–19.
5. Tony Manzi et al., eds., Social Sustainability in Urban Areas: Communities, Connectivity and the Urban Fabric (London: EarthScan, 2010), 49–63.
6. Maryam Keramati Ardakani and Seyyed Saeed Ahmadi Oloonabadi, "Collective Memory as an Efficient Agent in Sustainable Urban Conservation," *Procedia Engineering* 21 (2011): 985–988.
7. UNESCO (United Nations Educational, Scientific and Cultural Organization), World Heritage Centre, New Life for Historic Cities: The Historic Urban Landscape Approach Explained, 2013, 16–17.
8. Sarah Court and Gamini Wijesuriya, "People-centered Approaches to the Conservation of Cultural Heritage: Living Heritage," International Centre for the Study of the Preservation and Restoration of Cultural Property, 2015.

Figure Credits
Figure 1: Historical images of Datong Road, from 1930 to 1980 (photos courtesy of Meizhang Photo Studio, Xiamen, China).
Figure 2: Yingping District, 2021 (authors' photos).
Figure 3: Recycle framework for regeneration (authors' diagram).
Figure 4: Heritage space and buildings within the selected research area in Yingping District (created by An Hong Jie, member of authors' research team).
Figure 5: Planning strategy for the selected study area in Yingping District adapted to the recycle framework for regeneration (authors' diagram).
Figure 6: The process of planning an intervention for the sharing and regeneration of a heritage space in old urban quarters (authors' diagram).
Figure 7: Optimized strategy for reshaping the rich experience in Old Theatre Plaza (created by Wu Yun Jie, member of authors' research team).
Figure 8: Unitilization of historical buildings in Meditation Street (created by Li Xi Da, member of authors' research team).
Figure 9: Design for Haoyue Temple (authors' diagram).
Figure 10: Core space design of Red Street (designed by An Hong Jie, member of authors' research team).
Figure 11: Planning of Citizen Life Route and Cultural Experience Route (authors' diagram).

34

The House of Remembrance Singapore Residence

Entrance to the house

Architect firm: Neri&Hu Design and Research Office, K2LD (local architect)
Principal architect: Lyndon Neri, Rossana Hu
Senior Associate-in-charge: Christine Chang
Design team: Sela Lim, Bella Lin, Kevin Chim, Alexander Goh, Haiou Xin, July Huang
Location: Singapore
Area: 1,185.20 square meters
Completion date: December 2021
Photography: Fabian Ong

The traditional Chinese courtyard house or *siheyuan* is a typology well-known for its illustration of Confucian ideals, and it accommodates extended family units so many generations may live under one roof. To live under the same roof means to live together, and this metaphor is the nexus that ties the notion of community, especially in an intimate context, to the form crafted for this project.

For this private residence commission, the architects were given a set of unique requests by the client: The new house constructed in place of the previous one should accommodate all three siblings, who as adults have outgrown their shared house; it should include a small memorial space in the form of a garden for their late mother; and lastly, the new construction should retain the memory of the pitched-roof form, a defining feature of their old childhood home. The previous house was built in the style of a

British colonial bungalow with hybrid elements like deep eaves to shelter from rain (abstracted from traditional Malay houses), as well as Victorian details. Understanding the functional importance of the roof and the client's emotional attachment to its form, the design combines the pitched roof with a reinterpretation of the courtyard house.

This project explores how notions of communal living and collective memory can be expressed spatially. The new two-story house organizes all communal spaces around a central garden, which occupies the courtyard space that serves as a memorial garden for the family's late matriarch. The original lush green buffer along the perimeter is retained so the ground level is extroverted in nature, with expansive glass walls to connect all spaces to the garden along the edge of the site. Visual transparency is maximized in the communal areas—living room, open kitchen, dining room, and study—such that inhabitants may look into the central memorial garden from most areas on the ground floor cocooned by the dense vegetation surrounding the house. Large sliding glass doors promote cross ventilation and allow direct access to the gardens.

In the upper level, the idea of the pitched-roof form is pursued, not only as a symbol of shelter, but also as an element that both unifies and demarcates the public and private realms. All private bedrooms, located on the upper introverted level, are

housed within the roof's steep gables, so that when seen from the exterior, the house retains the appearance of a single-story hipped-roof bungalow. Skylights and large glass walls connect to bedroom balconies where views are orientated toward the perimeter garden. Through sectional interplay, three double-height areas to connect the communal functions and the corridors above are introduced. These spaces of interpenetration create vertical visual connections to allow one to peer into the public realm from the private.

The roof volume is interrupted by a carved void that frames a small tree before leading to the central memorial garden. On the exterior, where balconies and sky-wells are carved out from the volume of the pitched-roof form, the walls transition from smooth to board-formed concrete, reflecting the natural grain of wooden planks. The circulation on the ground floor is based on the shape of a circle to reinforce the circumambulatory experience of walking in a circular direction, and to define the memorial space as a sacred element. Since the circle has no edges or terminating vantage points, it allows one to always find a return to the center, both spiritually and physically. The garden symbolically defines the heart of the home as an ever-palpable void, persisting as the common backdrop to the collective lives of the home's inhabitants.

The carved void in the roof volume frames a small tree

Site plan

The memorial garden

Large glass doors

Circular corridor surrounding the memorial garden

The memorial space is defined as a sacred element in the center of the circular corridor

Visual transparency within the communal areas

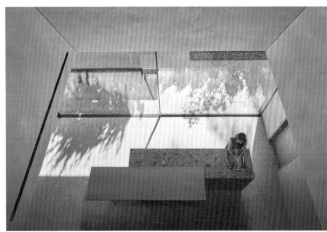

Peering into the public realm

Bedrooms in the upper level

Double-height area

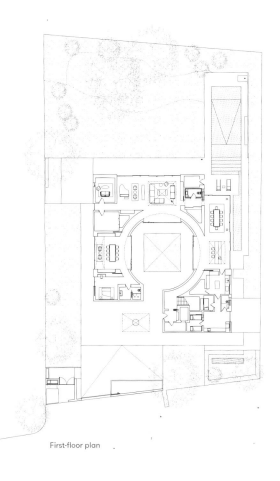

First-floor plan

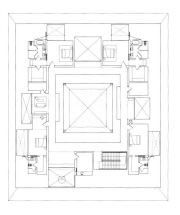

Second-floor plan

New swimming pool

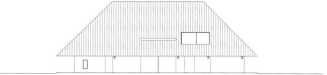

North elevation

West elevation

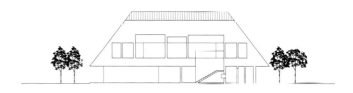

Cross sections

Greenery Curtain House

The front of the house is covered with green trees to block the sun, dust, and noise

Architecture firm: HGAA
Principal architect: Nguyen Van Thu
Design team: Tran Mai Phuong,
Vu An Tuan Minh, Nham Huy Hieu
Location: Mao Khe, Quang Ninh Province,
Vietnam
Area: 400 square meters
Completion date: December 2019
Photography: Duc Nguyen

The house is built in Mao Khe, a growing economic belt in Quang Ninh Province, Vietnam that has many urban constructions. Quang Ninh Province was also a mining center that extracted mineral coal and this had left the area in a bad shape with a low environmental quality. However, in recent years, as air quality improved and the urban landscape began to take shape, the condition of the area got better.

The owners of the house is an elderly couple that is accustomed to a simple, quiet life, except on weekends, when their family visits. The project creates a house that is close to nature and which displays a fresh atmosphere. The weight of the design is focused on the garden, the fish pond, and the architectural space.

The house flows from outside to inside around red brick walls that organize spaces (both exterior and interior) canopied by trees and lush greenery. The home's green elements are presented in different layers, such as shade trees, shrubs, and creepers that hang down from the roof, forming a "curtain" that prevents dust and noise from the outside filtering in. A main floor combines with a small space above for reading and worship; living spaces are arranged around an inner courtyard in the middle of the house, creating a peaceful, quiet radial space that is separate from the city outside. The spaces in the house are surrounded by nature and orientated toward nature. As they face each other, they form an introverted space, helping to connect people with nature, people with each other, and people with themselves. From every position in the house, people can see each other, trees and greenery, the waterbody, and the pond; in this house, one experiences nature in the form of air, sound, and light.

The main materials used in the house are red bricks and bare concrete, which create a rustic, cozy, and humanistic character. The correct use of materials will help define the architectural space, evoke emotions in people, and create a connection between them and the space, as well as enhance the beauty of the space and its surrounding nature. In this project, simple methods and common local materials create a living space full of emotion, and one that is close to people and nature.

From a distance, the house is a simple cube, contrasting with neighboring houses while not being too prominent

The spacious porch helps to block the sun and rain, and connects the outside to the indoor space, as well as acts as a buffer against the home's surroundings

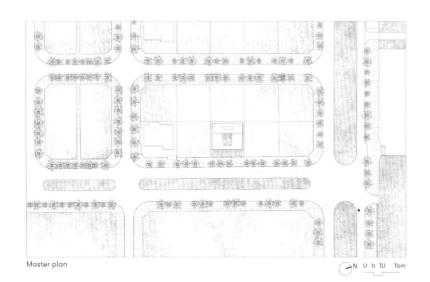

Master plan

N 0 5 10 15m

Rows of vines forming a natural green curtain

The garden space is located in the center, and is quiet and separate from the home's semi-outdoor area

View of the front of the house from the outside in the evening

Living room space overlooking nature

The calm, spacious dining room overlooks the garden

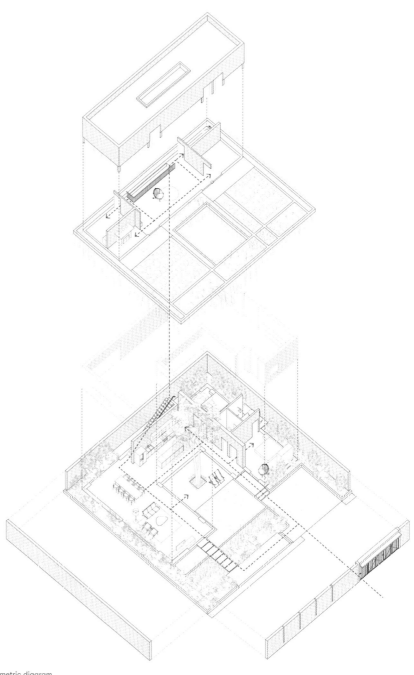

Isometric diagram

View from living room to garden

Kitchen space

Extra bedroom

Main bedroom

Main bedroom overlooking the pond

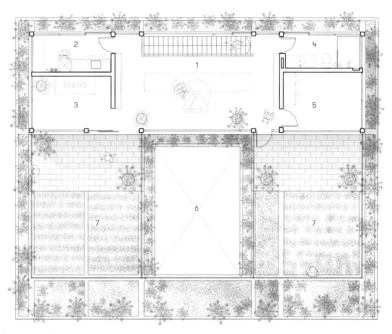

Second-floor plan

1. Reading space
2. Laundry
3. Altar
4. Bathroom
5. Bedroom
6. Void
7. Vegetable garden

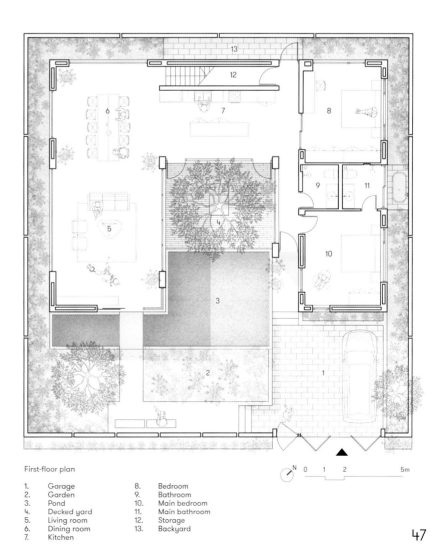

First-floor plan

1. Garage
2. Garden
3. Pond
4. Decked yard
5. Living room
6. Dining room
7. Kitchen
8. Bedroom
9. Bathroom
10. Main bedroom
11. Main bathroom
12. Storage
13. Backyard

N   0   1   2   5m

Reading and relaxing space upstairs

Rooftop vegetable garden

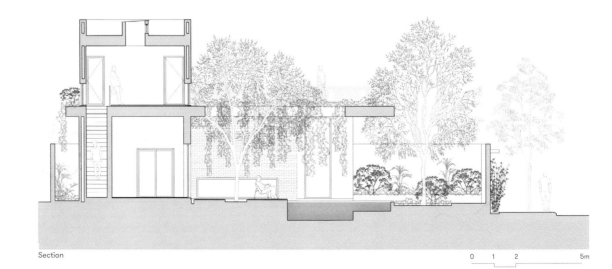

Section

0   1   2   5m

Tonami Public Libro

The library is a new landmark of Tonami City with its large, gently undulating roof

Architect firm: MIKAMI Architects, Oshida
Architects & Engineers Co., Ltd
Principal architect: Kazuhiko Mashiko
Design team: MIKAMI Architects
Location: Tonami City, Toyama Prefecture,
Japan
Area: 6,602.24 square meters
Completion date: July 2020
Photography: Kouji Horiuchi

This public library is located in Tonami City, Toyama Prefecture, Japan, facing the Sea of Japan.

Scattered Settlements and *Azumadachi*
The wide, open, and tranquil fields of Tonami once produced various types of grains for Kaga Hyakumangoku, the wealthy Kaga Domain of the Edo period. The breathtaking rural landscape, known as *sankyoson* or scattered settlements has been inherited through the ages, and people who have been living here for generations have much emotional attachment to the area, which translates as a rich spirit and a high level of

Library entrance seen from the north: wooden ceiling extends to the outside to welcome visitors

dignity and rationality. This attachment and pride extend to the region's traditional wooden farmhouse architecture that dominates the landscape. Known as *azumadachi*, these traditional farmhouses that surround the site inspired the design of the Tonami Public Library. The look and feel of the main building references the *azumadachi* in an open-plan space housed beneath a large timber roof, therein actualizing the project's design concept of "the one-roomed library under a large roof."

The Large Roof as a Landmark
The large, gentle wave in the massive roof is a modern interpretation of the traditional *azumadachi* and is reminiscent of the wings of a Pegasus as it soars in the sky. It is hoped that this roof structure will become a new landmark in Tonami City, and that in the years to come, the library will be regarded by the public as a symbol of refinement. The layout of the building is arranged such that the road along its west runs parallel to the low-hanging roof eaves to reveal the inside of the building through floor-to-ceiling glazing to passing traffic and passers-by.

Interior Space Drawn With a Single Stroke of the Brush
The space inside the building is the inversion of the gentle wave of the large roof and reveals that both are connected as one. The north side, which houses one of the library's two entrances, is often busier than the other areas on account of the crowds of people that stop by for short visits. As you go deeper, the steep slant of the ceiling at the entrance

transforms into a gentle timber slope patterned like radiating sun rays, creating another dimension in the visual perception of the space. High windows allow natural light to pour in freely, embracing visitors in a warm, inviting ambiance that is also serene and visually engaging.

A two-way staircase leads to the upper level and offers an unimpeded view of the entire interior; it also slyly reveals the magnified mosaic tulip pattern on the ground-floor carpet to the observant eye as one ascends the stairs.

A Library Where Citizens Can Participate
Even though libraries are among public facilities that are used regularly and continuously, conventional libraries are often used only by an estimated half of the population. In the first five months of its opening, Tonami Public Library recorded about 10,000 visitors in spite of the Covid epidemic, reflecting the success of the facility. A range of activities have been organized to engage with citizens, which includes picture book reading sessions for children, lectures, and many other events in which all ages of people can participate, keeping alive the community spirit and the strength of the community. Special exhibits are also often featured, taking advantage of the large display shelves. Volunteers were also recruited when the library opened, and to date, more than sixty people have supported and contributed to library operations by creating POP (point of purchase) signs, distributing books, and tending to the flowers and trees on the site.

49

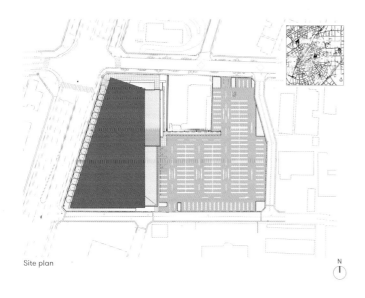
Site plan

N

Sign at entrance welcoming people who approach from the national highway; the three-color logo was designed in the image of the Tonami City emblem based on the city's national flower, the tulip

The library, as seen from the national highway: the open-racks area on the second floor is visible and overlooks the inviting ambiance of the first floor of the library

Service desk at entrance welcomes visitors—signage featuring the tulip, the national flower of Tonami City, is displayed throughout the entrance area and library

The library can be seen in its entirety from the north entrance

A panoramic view of the library interior from the south side of the second floor—the ceiling of the large, gently undulating roof is finished with cedar planks in a radial arrangement and the high window on the east side allows soft natural light into the entire interior

First-floor open-racks space viewed from the second-floor reading area—the wooden ceiling gently slopes toward the open-racks space on the first floor, fluidly connecting the second floor and the first floor

Wood combined with the soft, natural light filtering in through the high windows creates a warm, inviting atmosphere that is contrasted and given an edge with the reflective mirror surface on the side of the bookshelves

A low ceiling in the children's open-racks area fashions a cozy enclave that children flock to

The reading area in the children's open-racks section is arranged along the west side facing the main street with colorful and inviting furniture, such as chairs with tulip-shaped backrests, to add interest and liveliness

The partition between the entrance hall and the multipurpose conference room can be fully opened to allow them to be used together for exhibitions

Reading and study seats on the second floor gently connect to the first floor

A large and a small meeting room in the "Space for Meetings and Exhibitions" section

The Silent Room, usually used for quiet study

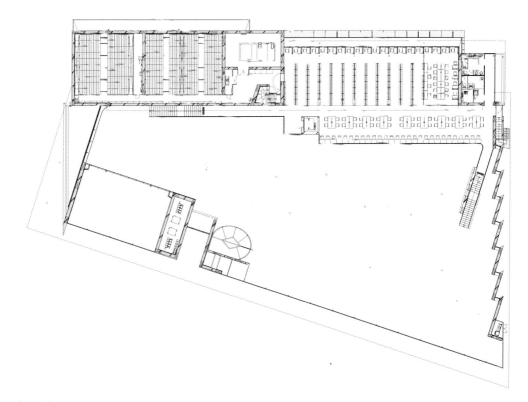

Second-floor plan

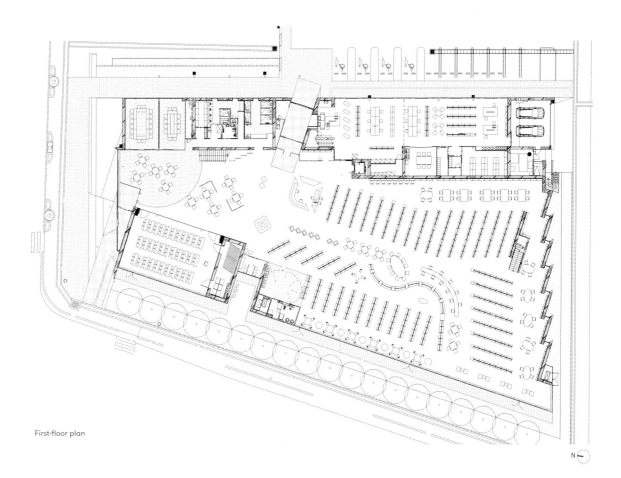

First-floor plan

N

Rear exterior of the Library

The unique design of Tonami Public Library allows it to reveal many different sides that add layered dimensions to the library experience

North elevation

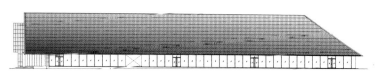

West elevation

Cross sections

Chapel of Sound

Rough concrete exterior

Architect firm: OPEN Architecture
Principal architect: Li Hu, Huang Wenjing
Design team: Zhou Tingting, Fang Kuanyin,
Huang Zetian, Lin Bihong, Jia Han,
Chen Xiuyuan, Cai Zhuoqun, Kuo Chunchen,
Tang Ziqiao
Location: Chengde, Hebei Province, China
Area: 790 square meters
Completion date: October 2021
Photography: Jonathan Leijonhufvud, Zhu
Runzi, Ni Nan

Nestled in a mountainous valley two hours away by car from the center of Beijing, the Chapel of Sound is a monolithic open-air concert hall with views to the ruins of the Ming dynasty's Great Wall. Designed to look like a boulder that had seemingly toppled from a mountain face and gently rolled into place in that spot, the building is built entirely from concrete that is enriched with an aggregate of local mineral-rich rocks. Encompassing a semi-outdoor amphitheater, an outdoor stage, viewing platforms, and a green room, the Chapel of Sound has been designed to offer the uncommon and deeply moving experience of listening to music performed right in the cradle of nature. The architects also hope that it can serve as a place where people can settle down and just listen to the sound of nature around them, which they believe is profoundly inspiring and healing. When there is no performance,

the concert hall is also a tranquil space for contemplation and community gatherings, with stunning views of the sky and the surrounding landscape.

To minimize the footprint of the concert hall in the valley, the structure rests in dialogue with the captivating natural landscape, though it is not of nature. The rock-like form is composed of an inner and outer shell, with the space between operating like a truss, and it was ultimately achieved through a close collaboration with international engineering firm Arup. Formed from concrete, each striation cantilevers out from the previous layer to create the inverted cone shape. Winding staircases weave through the building to a rooftop platform that offers panoramic views of the valley and the Great Wall. In the interior spaces, bronze accents in details such as handrails and doors create a warm contrast against the concrete.

The open project brief allowed ample room for the design team to be inspired, as well as to research all aspects of performance, particularly considering how the behaviors of sound can be a driving force behind the final shape of a building; specifically, to visually "see the shape of sound." The different ways that sound reverberates in natural spaces—such as caves—was ultimately the hook that conceptualized the design. Having designed theaters and concert halls, the team was

aware that the challenge in this project would lie in creating an excellent acoustic environment without introducing additional sound absorbing materials. Working with acoustic engineers, the design team reviewed the many ways in which people would usually experience sound in a concert hall, and defined openings that act as both sound absorption areas and connectors with the exterior environment.

Recognizing that humanity today, more than ever, is questioning its relationship with nature, and that it's important for people to be humble and take time to hear what nature is saying, the architects sought to create a place where people can experience the symphony of nature.

There is an inherent air of mystery around the Chapel of Sound that draws one in on the approach itself. This extends to how people will interact with the space—from it being a place for individual reflection, to a venue for large-scale concerts, the structure can be experienced in many different ways. The architects aspired for the definition of the space to avoid being absolute, so as to make room for all possibilities. Whether the space is experienced in solitude or in the company of others, or whether it is utilized for listening to music, the sound of nature, or gazing into the starry sky or connecting with one's inner self, the Chapel of Sound is open to the interpretation of the user.

The building is nestled at the bottom of a valley

The building "treads" the ground with a small footprint

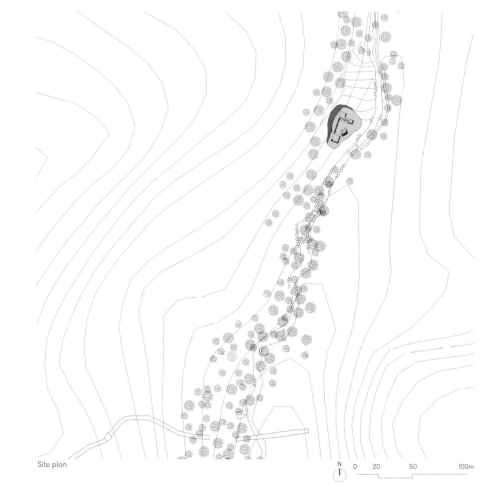
Site plan

N   0   20   50   100m

Valley covered in snow

Opening in the roof

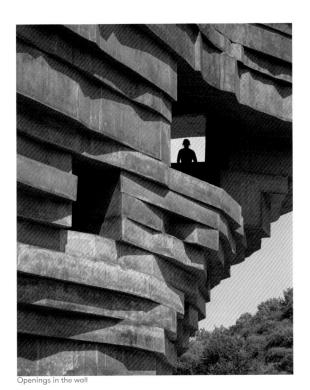
Openings in the wall

59

Semi-outdoor amphitheater—night view

Stairway

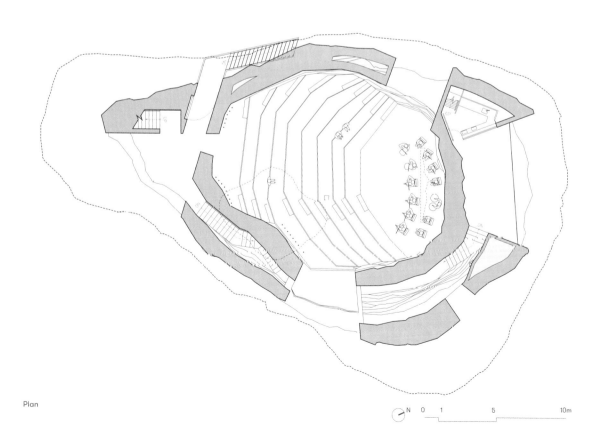

Plan

N   0   1   5   10m

Valley view terrace

Semi-outdoor amphitheater

61

Outdoor stage facing a gentle slope

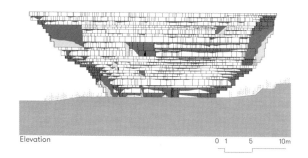

Elevation

0 1   5   10m

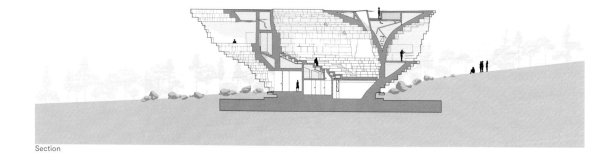

62

Section

Phetkasem Artist Studio

The soil sprayed steel pipe bricks used in the façade is the first development and use of such a technology in Thailand

Architect firm: HAS Design and Research
Principal architect: Jenchieh Hung, Kulthida Songkittipakdee
Design team: HAS Design and Research, Pacific Pipe Co. Ltd, Goldstar Metal Co. Ltd.
Location: Bangkok, Thailand
Area: 150 square meters
Completion date: January 2021
Photography: Ketsiree Wongwan

Phetkasem Artist Studio, hidden in a residential suburb in Bangkok, Thailand, has been built in the typical townhouse architecture style of Thailand. This commercial housing typology was mass-produced by developers thirty years ago and had instantly spread to numerous capital cities in Southeast Asia, creating a kind of a sense of indifference in Thailand's cityscapes. In Phetkasem Village, however, the residents exhibited a different lifestyle from those in typical residential units in other areas.

They built fences to create a larger garage area, extended the roofs of their homes in front of their houses over footpaths to increase storage space, and extended rain sheds to enable ground-level commercial possibilities. They also used potted plants, which sometimes even obstructed the roads, to satisfy their vision of small gardens. These "improvised" yet harmonious artificial structures featured, in particular, materials made of metal, such as steel pipes and iron rods. These metal components were not only used for material structure and shape, but also used in large amounts in daily illegal constructions in Bangkok (like overhanging signage and awnings over the street). The result of this illicit practice is known as "readily available steel pipes/iron rods in Thailand."

Thailand was once a major steel producer and the largest exporter of steel pipes in Southeast Asia. However, these materials lost their fundamental purpose when they became overused in advertising signs, balcony windows, rain shelters, and such alternative offhanded constructions.

While steel pipes have become "ordinary," coming off as uninspiring, they still bear some unique traits that can create interesting aspects if used to their potential. In the eyes of the design team, the most captivating features of the many steel pipes glinting everywhere in the streets of Thailand are their elegant curvature and their light, hollow shape. Unfortunately, so far, these characteristics have yet to be effectively adopted in a construction. So, for this project, playing off the vibe of the village's shanty constructions, the design team collaborated with Pacific Pipe, a well-known Thai steel pipe producer, to use steel pipes as unit bricks to create "steel pipe bricks." Displaying a height and width close to 4 meters, the steel pipe bricks produce the microclimate effects of sunshade lighting and convection ventilation. The design also employs a half-split steel pipe on both sides of the unit, so that pipes of five different diameters are integrated into the same unit to create a variety of mixed-effects through rotation and mirroring. The special steel pipe bricks manufactured for this project also mark the first time in Thailand that steel pipe bricks have been combined with soil texture spraying technology—which is an acrylic resin-based product that uses spray painting to cover heated steel material in the same color and texture as soil—creating low energy cost and convective ventilation effects, thereby providing an alternative residential lifestyle in the tropical climate.

Site plan

N 0 5 10 20m

In the entrance space of the building, these unique steel pipe bricks form a quiet semi-open area that brings in light breezes; set in the lush surroundings of Thailand's native trees, a unique arrival experience is created.

The design connects the front yard with the backyard through apertures in the brick system; with no air-conditioning system installed on the first floor, and an especially enduring tropical climate of nearly 40°C, this regulates the interior climate by introducing alley breezes into the living environment, thereby also tailoring a new type of lifestyle closer to nature.

The second-floor area intentionally exposes the original column-beam structure, which emphasizes the non-conventional sense of scale produced by a vast difference between the width and height of the pitched roof, contrasting the atmospheres of the compact first floor and the spacious second floor.

Phetkasem Artist Studio is not only a workspace for artistic creation, but also a residence that combines living, resting, and dining functions. Its form breaks the image of Thailand's typical commercial housing building, and through the region's common industrial materials, it reshapes a new building type that combines geography, climate, and the surrounding neighborhood. On this project, the design team cooperated with multiple international consultants across the globe, including steel curtain wall consultant Pacific Pipe, aluminum door and window consultant Goldstar Metal, lighting technology company Visual Feast, sanitaryware consultant American Standard, landscape consultant FloraScape, and signage consultant Shanghai View Studio. The architect believes that this renovation of an old building with structural and size limitations can be a driving force for an innovative change. This building is now better equipped for practical use, with retrospection into the past and prospection into the future.

The design brings freedom to the space as it connects and separates the private space on the second floor and the art space on the first floor

Rear view of Phetkasem Artist Studio

The gravel road mimics a winding path in a traditional Thai alley

The calm courtyard creates a peaceful and unusual arrival experience in the bustling city

The cascading holed walls block excessive sunlight and street noise

The floating wall allows for breezes to connect from the front courtyard to the backyard, providing good air circulation

Art craft area

Interior breezeway

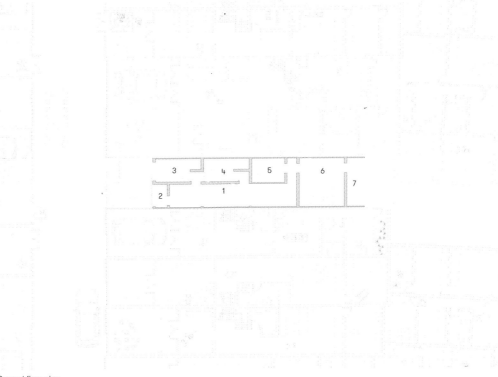

Second-floor plan

1.   Event space
2.   Balcony
3.   Reading collection
4.   Bathroom
5.   Walk-in closet
6.   Main bedroom
7.   Terrace

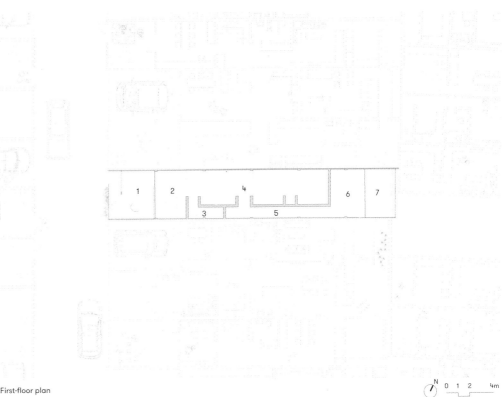

First-floor plan

1.   Hidden gravel yard
2.   Multifunctional space
3.   Bathroom
4.   Art production space
5.   Gallery corridor
6.   Dining space
7.   Bamboo forest

N 0 1 2   4m

The interior space exudes a sense of timelessness

Curved holes of different sizes introduce natural breezes for air circulation and replace the need for air conditioning indoors

The design transforms from holes to a variety of door openings for a more flexible use of the second-floor space

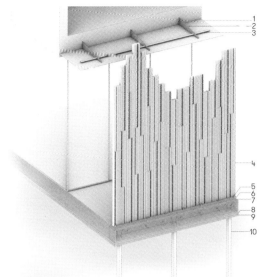

Isometric diagram—detail of back wall

1. 2mm aluminum panel
2. 50–200 mm T-steel
3. φ 20 mm steel bar
4. Pipe wall
5. L-bolt 500 mm
6. Base plate 12 mm
7. Non-shrink grout
8. Lean concrete 50 mm THK
9. Compact sand 50 mm THK
10. Pile φ 150×6,000 mm

The wall has a unique bamboo-like texture

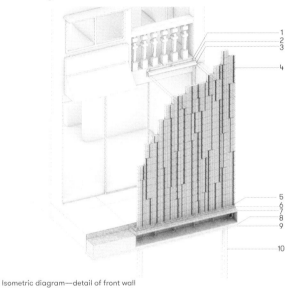

Isometric diagram—detail of front wall

1. Stud bolt 1/2"
2. Steel plate 12 mm THK
3. C-steel 75×75×9 mm
4. Pipe wall
5. L-bolt 50 mm
6. Base plate 12 mm
7. Non-shrink grout
8. Lean concrete 50 mm THK
9. Compact sand 50 mm THK
10. Pile φ 150×6,000 mm

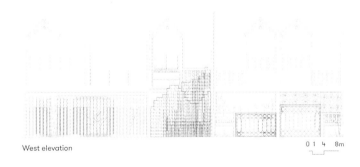

West elevation

0 1 4 8m

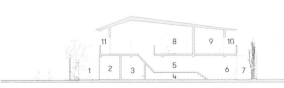

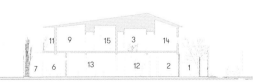

Sections

0 1 2 4m

1. Hidden gravel yard
2. Multifunctional space
3. Bathroom
4. Storage
5. Gallery corridor
6. Dining space
7. Bamboo forest
8. Event space
9. Main bedroom
10. Balcony
11. Terrace
12. Library
13. Art production space
14. Art book collection
15. Walk-in closet

The Pilot Section of Maozhou River Ecological Belt

Ring of Blueway

Architect firm: Tongji Architectural Design
(Group) Co., Ltd (TJAD)
Principal architect: Zhang Ming, Lou Huiling,
Cheng Wei, Liu Zujian
Design team: Yuan Tianyuan, Zhang Wei,
Qiu Wenmin, Li Xiubing, Xi Qing, Zhang Zi,
Qin Shu, Jiang Du, Zhang Yu, Luo Xi, Yang Xiu,
Jiang Puhai, Yu Ping, Tian Lijun
Location: Shenzhen, China
Area: 12.9 km (total length); 15.5 km² (total
planning area)
Completion date: September 2020
Photography: Tianjian Studio

As the "mother river" of Shenzhen, China, Maozhou River has witnessed many significant events in Shenzhen's history, one of them being the region's rapid rise from a small border town into an international metropolis with global influence.

However, alongside this ascend was also a contrary descend. Over the last thirty years, as the region worked toward its progress, many urban villages and small factories had gathered on both sides of the Maozhou River, which led to domestic sewage being discharged directly into the river. This caused the river to deteriorate rapidly from a life-giving river as the villagers' source of drinking water, to a black and smelly river that was eagerly avoided by the citizens. At the end of 2015, Shenzhen launched an extensive campaign to control and prevent water pollution, and four years later, after the river had time to cleanse itself and repair, the water quality of the Maozhou River finally reached the "V standard" for surface water, indicating the complete elimination of black, malodorous water.

To take things further, at the end of 2019, the Shenzhen government announced their anti-pollution vision for the region's water networks themed "quality river, quality riversides," in response to the call of the Wanli Bidao water network project in Guangdong Province. TJAD participated in the planning and implementation of the pilot section of the Wanli Bidao project, the Bidao Maozhou River.

The pilot section extends about 12.9 kilometers long (the Bao'an section is about 6.1 kilometers long and the Guangming section is about 6.8 kilometers long), with the overall planning area being about 15.5 square kilometers. The design idea was to base the pilot section on the road network and the status quo of the spatial structure, but by using water as the main line instead. Through regional ecological environment optimization, composite space utilization, and improved industrial structure and urban function transformation, the construction sets flood discharge channels, ecological corridors, leisure and cultural trains, as well as industrial chains, which integrate a high quality waterfront space as the model of shared governance of "water, industry, and city."

Relying on their "talent" network, the design team gathered teams for planning, landscape, architecture, municipal administration, bridge engineering, and so on, so as to provide integrated and comprehensive services for the project. Through river regulation, ecological resilience and water system security resilience can be built to solve the problems of ecological restoration and flood storage; through urban spatial governance, industrial resilience and economic development resilience can be built to enhance the intervention of government, community, and local industries. This project not only realizes the original intention of "returning the river to the people," but it is also an important strategy to activate urban human resources and improve urban identifiability.

Daweisha River commercial street

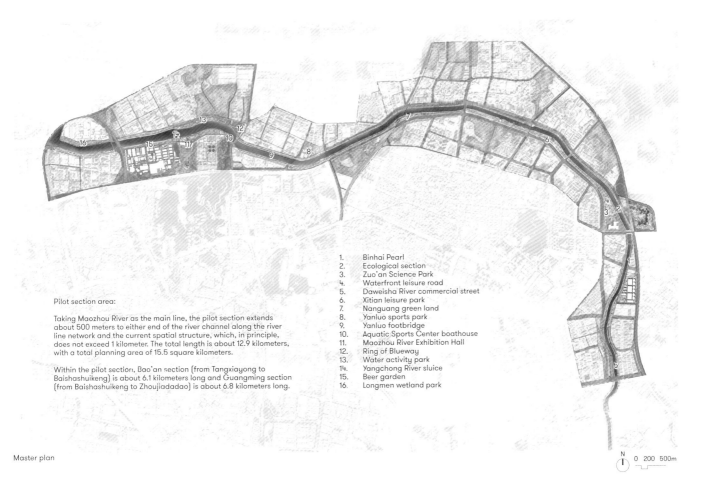

Pilot section area:

Taking Maozhou River as the main line, the pilot section extends about 500 meters to either end of the river channel along the river line network and the current spatial structure, which, in principle, does not exceed 1 kilometer. The total length is about 12.9 kilometers, with a total planning area of 15.5 square kilometers.

Within the pilot section, Bao'an section (from Tangxiayong to Baishashuikeng) is about 6.1 kilometers long and Guangming section (from Baishashuikeng to Zhoujiadadao) is about 6.8 kilometers long.

1. Binhai Pearl
2. Ecological section
3. Zuo'an Science Park
4. Waterfront leisure road
5. Daweisha River commercial street
6. Xitian leisure park
7. Nanguang green land
8. Yanluo sports park
9. Yanluo footbridge
10. Aquatic Sports Center boathouse
11. Maozhou River Exhibition Hall
12. Ring of Blueway
13. Water activity park
14. Yangchong River sluice
15. Beer garden
16. Longmen wetland park

Master plan

N   0 200 500m

Binhai Pearl

Ecological section

Zuo'an Science Park

Waterfront leisure road

Nanguang green land

Maozhou River Exhibition Hall

Terraced wetland

Ring of Blueway

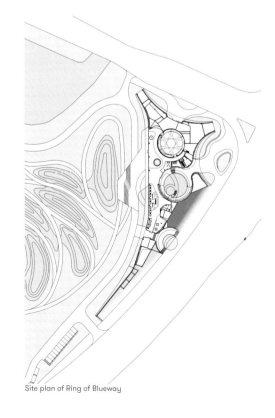
Site plan of Ring of Blueway

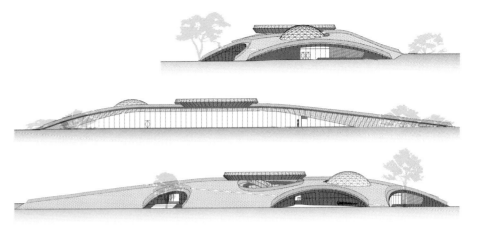

Elevations

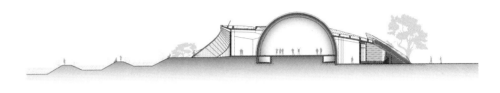

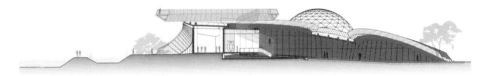

Sections

Ring of Blueway

75

Water activity park

Yangchong River sluice

Beer garden

Longmen wetland park

Park Hyatt Niseko Hanazono, Chapel

View of the eastern elevation from the waterscape

Architect firm: Nikken Sekkei Ltd, Fujita Corporation
Principal architect: Kagami Ado
Design team: Miyuki Chiba, Ishii Takako
Location: Iwaobetsu, Kutchan Town, Abuta-gun, Hokkaido, Japan
Area: 283 square meters
Completion date: November 2019
Photography: Kouji Horiuchi, Shin Shashin Koubou

Opened in January 2020, Park Hyatt Niseko Hanazono is a luxury mountain resort located in the pristine heart of Niseko's Hanazono area in Hokkaido, Japan, and operates year-round. A renowned international winter ski resort, it also offers seasonal outdoor activities such as hiking, mountain biking, and river rafting during non-winter months.

The resort's chapel is located in the functional village built around a courtyard that is separate from guestroom facilities, and reflects harmonious Japanese aesthetics in its design. Its "floating grand roof" is symbolic of traditional Japanese architecture and helps to achieve a feeling of openness in its interior. Measuring 20 meters in length, the roof effectively blurs the boundary between indoor and outdoor areas.

With a pristine birch forest in the background and ample space between the front garden pond and the backyard, guests can enjoy a semi-outdoor resort experience, complete with a seasonal shift in scenery. The depth of the artificially created pond is adjustable and can be configured to yield an outdoor seating area suitable for concerts or other outdoor events.

Warm and elegant with neutral nuances, the chapel has been designed as a multipurpose facility equipped to host private dining occasions for guests, buffets, seminars, conferences, and concerts.

Sliding doors that are a nod to the traditional Japanese *fusuma* (sliding opaque rectangular panels) allow a high degree of customizability. For example, by opening the chapel's 10-meter-long triple sliding doors, the nave (center portion) of the chapel can be extended to the outdoor stage area. Likewise, opening the entrance hall's 4-meter-wide double sliding doors allows it to also function as a foyer.

High side lighting between the two pitched roofs, along with stained glass positioned above the gable wall allow different expressions of light to enter, according to the prevailing climate, season, and time of day. Thick steel rods connect the roofs, which are supported by reinforced-concrete walls on both ends, leaving a 20-meter-long unobstructed space underneath.

In order to enhance the guest experience, mechanical and electrical equipment, such as the roof-embedded linear lighting fixtures, are hidden from view. Ceiling illumination lights, automated spotlights for the wedding aisle, and tall altar-side speakers are seamlessly camouflaged in fabric. The air conditioning system features an under-floor chamber to accommodate cold weather needs. It employs window-side air outlet grilles and concealed air-return inlets in a roller blind head box.

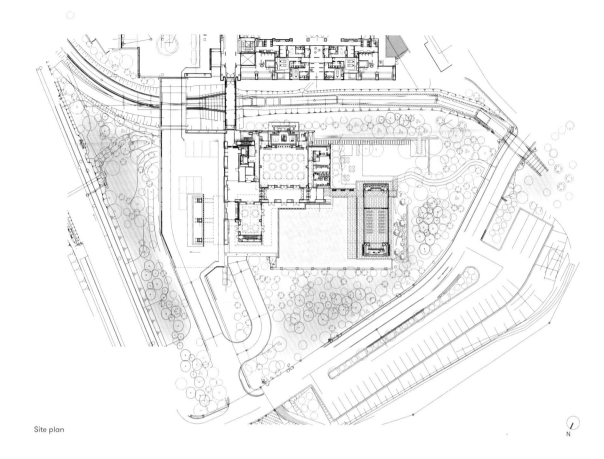

Site plan

N

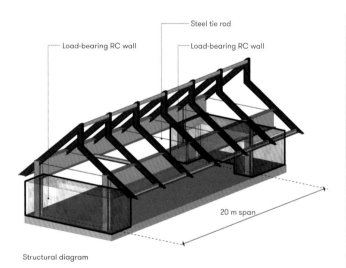

Steel tie rod

Load-bearing RC wall

Load-bearing RC wall

20 m span

Structural diagram

Aerial view of the fragmented roof

Night view from the passageway

Night view of the eastern elevation

Chapel's passageway

Chapel's foyer

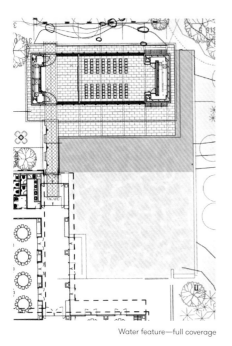
Water feature—full coverage

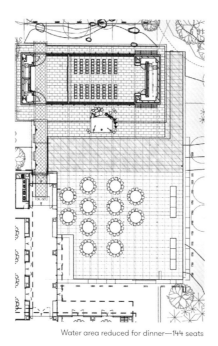
Water area reduced for dinner—144 seats

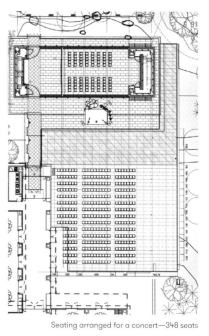
Seating arranged for a concert—348 seats

Resizable pond with outdoor seating—transforming from full-coverage to a smaller pond

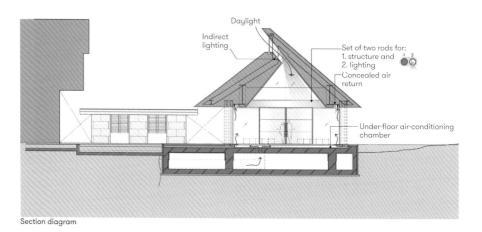
Section diagram

Zhangjiakou Library

Exterior view of Zhangjiakou Library

Architect firm: Tanzo Space Design Office
Principal architect: Wang Daquan
Design team: Tanzo Space Design Office,
Beijing Tsingshang Architectural Design and
Research Institute
Location: Hebei, China
Area: 22,200 square meters
Completion date: April 2021
Photography: Shi Yunfeng

Zhangjiakou Library—Creating the Spiritual Breath of the City

"To acquire the habit of reading is to construct for yourself a refuge."

W. Somerset Maugham

According to palaeolithic remains discovered, it is believed that the first populations in Zhangjiakou, Hebei Province, China, date back to almost a million years ago, and were made up of groups of people from different tribes and backgrounds who converged and multiplied in the town. They reclaimed the land, made their lives, and lived out their days here, and over time, set the precedent for Chinese civilizations that spread from this seed community. Since then, this piece of land has never been barren. Last year, Zhangjiakou displayed a new look to the world with the stylish, contemporary Zhangjiakou Library, which was constructed in time for the Beijing Winter Olympic Games in 2022.

Miniature Landscape
The Cohesion of City Humanism

Zhangjiakou is built close to mountains and rivers, and is surrounded on three sides—in the north, east, and west—by mountains. The Zhangjiakou Library, Archives, Museum, and Planning Museum are integrated into one

facility that is actualized in three volumes in the central canyon area. Open to the south, the massing of these volumes of different sizes is harmonious, even with their diversity in proportion. The building façade is covered by recyclable perforated panels and the entire building complex reflects like a miniature regional urban landscape with its contemporary artistic treatment.

Of the three buildings, the library on the east side is the largest, with a total construction area of 22,000 square meters. It contains a total book collection of about 1.1 million volumes and accommodates 2,100 reading seats. The open-shelf book displays are integrated with the reading area to promote the functions of collections display, searching, borrowing, and reading.

Less is not empty, but condensed; and more is not crowded, but appropriate. In this project, a prudent eye and an economic approach shape the core aesthetics; the architects abandon trivial and complicated decorations to optimize cost and make the design precise. The interior design follows the principle of systematic design and extends itself throughout the space based on the logic of architectural design.

Architecture is the art of artificial layering designed by the artist, and here, in the library, restrictions are released to create spaces for functional uses, that are with emotion and feeling. The overall building space adopts an integrated ceiling curtain wall that establishes the atrium. The platforms and main stairs on each floor define functional areas, as well as the interior's overall structural appearance, which is presented in a unifying gray and white color palette formed in concrete

cladding and timber. Light pours down through the ceiling's grid-frame curtain wall at different angles, creating different shades of layered light and shadow that add interest to the reading environment, and a sense of curiosity to the library experience.

Compound Space
Explaining Public Property of Library

The modern-day library is not only a place for storing books and borrowing them, but also a space where people gather to be inspired and interact socially. This behavior, through different scenarios, effortlessly converts the venue's functional purpose from being that of solely reading to include interacting as well. In urban life of the future, the library will become a link that connects people to knowledge, experience, and creation; within the city, it will explore the needs and possibilities of the community and stimulate the vitality of the generations, and even the landscape.

As the carrier of books, the library is sometimes abstract and sometimes concrete when the concept of books is integrated into the space. Ranging from the three scales of small, medium, and large, to the three light-and-dark levels of black, white, and gray, the design logic is based on the "two in one, three in two, and three in all" modular design. Books are arranged on shelves composed as lattices; as this connects the theme with visitors' interaction of the space, the interior presentation evolves from displaying as a two-dimensional plane into facilitating a three-dimensional space composition.

The pavement of the main library building's outdoor plaza is

81

extended and assembled with strips of light-hued, three-color terrazzo, which works in harmony with the building's holistic design; it also changes in arrangement organically, thereby effectively reducing material wastage that may occur with having to adhere to fixed repetitive design patterns, and also successfully integrates the interior and exterior spaces.

Visitors enter the library building through the main entrance located on the first floor. An independent volume in the center of the atrium, which reflects like a contemporary art installation, forms the multifunction hall, which is equipped to function as a small theater or a large lecture hall. Exhibiting an extremely upward sense, this volume, dressed in the design theme's lattice iteration, weakens the pressure of the atrium "chamber" formed by the rising building structure around it. As the focal point in the space, this multifunction hall is the heart of the program, pumping with vitality and releasing an active energy into the ambiance, activating yet stabilizing the entire space. The lattice elements in the skin of the volume are arranged in different orders and filled with high-quality sound-absorbing materials to effectively reduce noise filtering into the large space. An open, stepped square on the roof of the hall connects to the second floor. Planter boxes featuring tall plants are arranged on the steps in a dispersed and non-uniform ascending order to present a rich sense of visual hierarchy, especially when viewed against the background of the first floor. This seemingly random, but carefully designed arrangement also expands the perception of the traffic flow lines in the square, thereby appearing like a relatively open space when viewed within the full interior environment.

The façades of the three volumes feature a perforated curtain wall to negotiate the strong sunlight in Zhangjiakou. However, this renders the indoor light less suitable for reading, so the area close to the window is artfully designed as a promenade with a stage-like feel, with reading areas planned inward. The constantly changing light becomes a spotlight that illuminates the imaginary world of readers.

Cultural Aesthetics
Shape Social Value
Zhangjiakou Library expands the dimensions of people's artistic and literary life by shaping in-depth experiences of the interactions between human beings and architecture. It is equipped with a modern and intelligent management system to maintain public order, as well as patrons' safety at the entrance and exit points, and to also provide enhanced services like self-service storage facilities, library card application services, and information retrieval services through user-friendly LED screens. The convenience of advanced technology allows people to effortlessly obtain the information they need.

Spaces within the main library building are connected in a way that each space's position and moving line is assigned a different role. The open-space plan allows people of all ages and learning needs, with different purposes of visiting the library, to learn, interact, and gather together. The carefully considered division of the spaces promote multiple-way communication and provides ideal spatial situations for spontaneous encounters.

The youth reading area, as a high-frequency, high-use area is tailored to deliver a variety of artistic experiences. If one desires some leisure time in solitude, away from the rest of the crowd, the multidimensional video area and music room make the perfect spots. The children's area captures the most—and the best—natural light. Kids can read in cozy caves, enjoy audiovisual fun in the children's cinema, and explore and play safely.

Apart from specific functional areas, there are also areas reserved for other possibilities of future use. This is enabled by the transparency of the architectural material, which makes room for the possibility of hosting various activities; it reshapes the expression of the space through simultaneously "opening" and "closing" the wall. Adding to this, a modular composition allows the space the flexibility to be transformed into a gallery, concert hall, recording studio, event area, and so on.

Various activities that celebrate the region's history and culture have been staged at the Zhangjiakou Library. The private museum displays the historical documents of Zhangjiakou to give visitors a close look at the region's history of thousands of years. It displays the proper posture of a public building clearly and accurately without extra visual symbols and image features. This is the result of the architects' thorough contemplation of the atmosphere of the library building's interior and exterior spaces, and of considering possible future changes in urban life. "Architectures for books" are constantly developing and being upgraded, representing the never-ending spiritual construction of people and their cities. During the 2022 Winter Olympics, Zhangjiakou became an international meeting point pulsing with cultural communication, taking on the role of a seed that germinates to unite civilization, enlightening people in today's modern world.

Exterior

Night view of exterior of library building

Night view of library building façade

A small stepped square on the roof of the multifunction hall connects to the second floor

The pavement in the building's outdoor plaza is extended and assembled with strips of light and three-color terrazzo that is arranged in harmony with the holistic design to change organically, so as to reduce material wastage and effectively integrate interior and exterior spaces

84

Interior space of the library

Escalator located next to the multifunction hall

Corridor

As the lattice bookshelves connect the interior theme with visitors' interactions of the space, the interior arrangement evolves from displaying as a two-dimensional plane into facilitating a three-dimensional space composition

The library is equipped with a modern intelligent management system to provide services like self-service storage, membership application, and information retrieval

Film experience area (audio-visual corner)

Music appreciation area

The large lecture hall

86

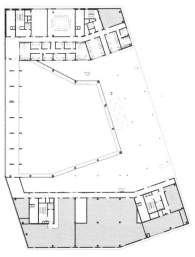

Fourth-floor plan

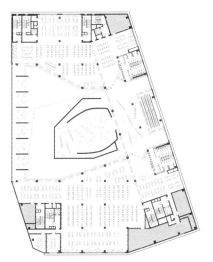

Second-floor plan

Third-floor plan

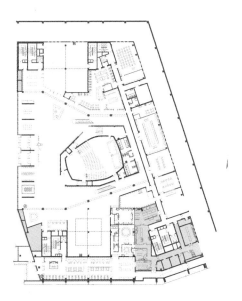

Lower-first-floor plan

First-floor plan

Youth reading area

Youth reading area

PROJECT

Takenaka Clinic

An L-shaped open-ceiling space achieves a "warm transparency"

Architect firm: TSC Architects
Principal architect: Yoshiaki Tanaka
Location: Aichi Prefecture, Japan
Area: 543 square meters
Completion date: November 2019
Photography: Hiroshi Tanigawa

A hospital usually tends to be a space that features drab colors and poor-quality construction materials that lack taste and materiality due to the use of artificial structure materials to improve the complex's functionality and efficiency. This cold and lack-luster ambiance often leads to patients feeling very diverted and separate from their day-to-day routines and comforts. The key to overcoming this is to provide more comfortable architectural spaces in medical facilities, where patients can spend their time without stress.

The client, a doctor who consults with more than 3,000 patients every month, envisioned a building that would exude the warmth of wood. However, this project did not embrace the design objective to simply construct a wooden hospital; no. It was a project driven by the desire to build a place where everyone who comes to the hospital can feel at ease. To satisfy the degree of freedom and performance of the plan, the design team uses a steel structure with an abundant amount of wood for the exterior and interior (partly also as an auxiliary to the structural material). Beyond visual aesthetics, the building's functional objective was also considered. In tandem with the building's purpose as a facility that connects medical services to the community, the building's architecture connects the inside and the outside, and the facility is designed as a clinic that exudes a sense of calm and openness.

The L-shaped atrium and large wooden eaves in this design play important roles. By planning an L-shaped atrium set street side, patients can experience a sense of openness. The waiting room is provided as a buffer space that connects the functions of the clinic with the community outside. The large wooden eaves serve as an approach space that welcomes patients, and also displays an ambiguous identity that is neither interior nor exterior, a concept known in Japan as

engawa—usually referring to the open exterior space under roof eaves in traditional Japanese houses. In this way, a warm and "transparent" clinic is realized.

Even though people don't usually visit a clinic unless they are ill, Takenaka Clinic flips the script and engages with local residents on a daily basis. The L-shaped atrium creates a transparent façade and as a result, internal activities and the warmth of the wooden interior are exposed to the city; and after the sun goes down, the clinic's lights share their bright illumination with the city, creating a strong presence on the site. Handmade tiles are used in the floor of the approach, creating a more personal, non-detached, non-generic ambiance often experienced in commercial or public establishments. The parking lot is also designed like a lawn floor using concrete blocks, creating a park-like atmosphere. A bench corner set up under the large wooden eaves provides a place for communicating, or can be a quiet place to rest.

The design of the clinic fulfills the doctor's wish that it should "serve as a base for health counseling," while also extending to the community the assurance of a reliable doctor nearby. It is hoped that this building will become the center of the town's community with its warm and inviting ambiance and its focus on reaching out to people.

89

The L-shaped atrium with its transparent façade results in the atrium's lights illuminating the city brightly after the sun goes down

Set adjacent to the street, the L-shaped open-ceiling atrium/waiting area has an open feel that is enhanced by the warm sunlight filtering in, rather than being an ominous enclosed area

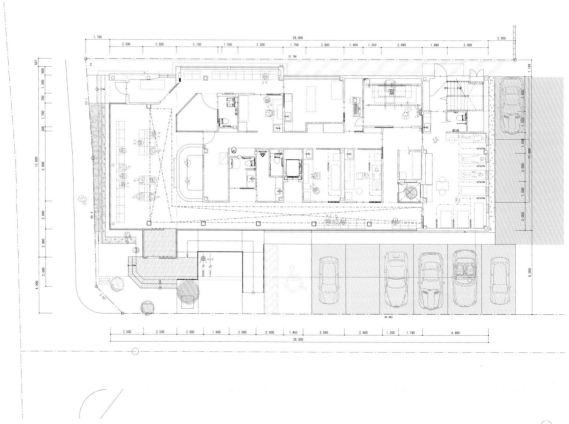

First-floor plan

N

The large wooden eaves create an ambiguous space that is neither interior nor exterior, a traditional edging/home veranda concept known in Japan as *engawa*

Wood is used in abundance in areas that directly interact with patients to reduce nervous energy and instill a sense of security and calmness

It is hoped the architecture will become the center of the community as it lends the warmth of its wooden component, while also displaying the clinic's activities within

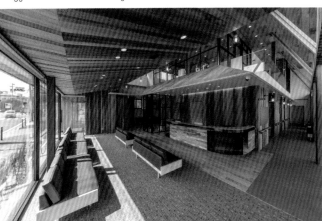

The L-shaped atrium connects the waiting room on the first floor and the rehabilitation room on the second floor, in addition to the outside and the inside

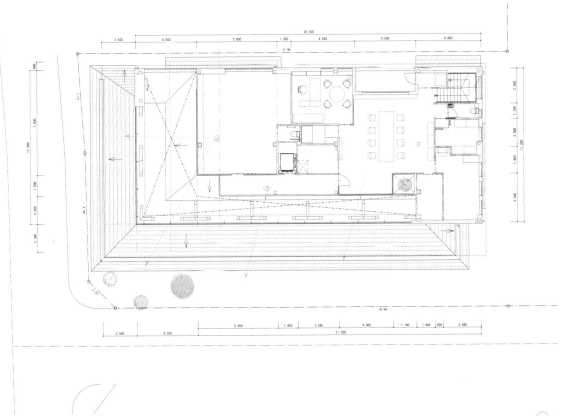

Second-floor plan

N

To configure the large eaves and the L-shaped open-ceiling space of the main waiting area, a steel structure with a brace is used, which also adds to the attractive aesthetics of the space

From the rehabilitation room, patients can view the cityscape outside through the L-shaped atrium

The L-shaped atrium not only connects the outside and inside of the clinic, but also connects the rehabilitation room on the second floor with the waiting room on the first floor

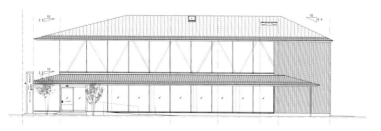

East elevation

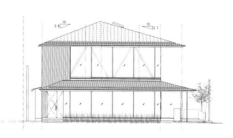

South elevation

The large wooden eaves serve as a warm approach space to welcome patients

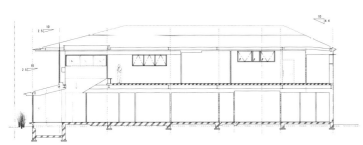
Section A-A

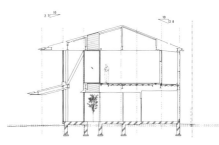
Section B-B

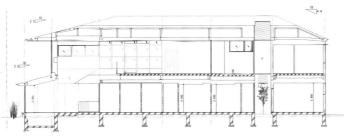
Section C-C

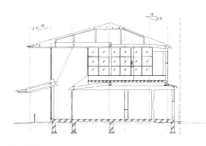
Section D-D

Stella Fiore

Aerial view of middle area of site

Architect firm: IROJE KHM Architects
Principal architect: HyoMan Kim
Design team: Kyungjin Chung, Seunghee Song,
Jiyeon Kim, Mihwa Oh, Ara Jo, Damhee Kim
Location: Seolmun-dong, IlsanDong-gu,
Goyang-si, Gyeonggi-do, South Korea
Area: 785.76 square meters
Completion date: November 2019
Photography: Sergio Pirrone

A Different World From the World

Crossing Stella Bridge, which stretches across a stream, where the boundary of the city lies, one enters the small town of Stella Fiore, which presents a perfect escape from the typical urban landscape and the stresses of modern society. Located here are Stella Fiore homes, a cluster of nineteen town houses primed and ready to offer a peaceful, yet contemporary dwelling that is a daily retreat from the urban hustle and bustle.

Stars Landed on Hill

To introduce sufficient sunlight and the beautiful, vibrant surrounding mountain views into the interior spaces in each house—composed of two main floors and two mezzanine levels—a "clear story" concept is employed, which installs roof-height windows framed in angled roofs. This design also protects the privacy of the interior and blocks it from the neighbors' sightlines, along with slanted walls that form part of the main mass. A split-level scheme arranges spaces in a zigzag layout that is contoured to match the incline line of the hillside site,

awarding unobstructed views of the surrounding natural forest that ensconces the homes.

Festive Hillside Village

Each house is separated by ample strolling space and walkways, fostering a positive communal lifestyle that is also private—by way of clever architecture that frames views of landscape scenery instead of your neighbor's house.

The main road leading to this cluster of unique homes is more than just a thoroughfare for vehicles and transportation. It's plaza-like characteristics mark it as a dynamic space for gathering and community activities among residents, creating opportunities to form a tight-knit resident community.

Small but Rich Space

The split-level interior layout arranges two main floors with two mezzanine levels that adapt seamlessly to the sloped hillside terrain. While the interior spaces may not be extravagant, they offer interesting experiences with their angled turns and tiered platforms to create unusual nooks and tucked-away spaces that contrast with open, revealed spaces, just waiting to be transformed into something extraordinary by a daring imagination.

Identification for Possessive Instinct

An embodiment of Korean culture itself, the nineteen homes in Stella Fiore are composed into three types of unit plans that are housed in four different eye-catching structural forms. The volumes are dressed in various-colored skins that are designed in aluminum, identifying the separate units as "one quirky individual."

Small court between two types of house design

Aerial view showing entrance gate

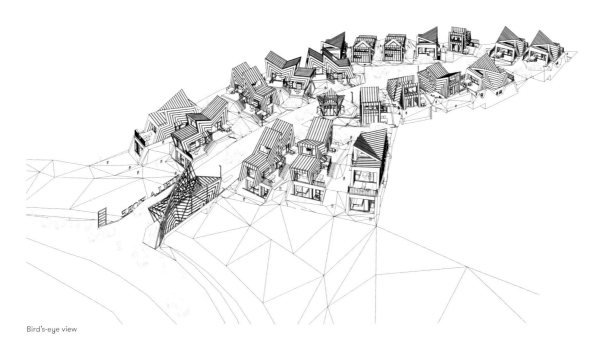
Bird's-eye view

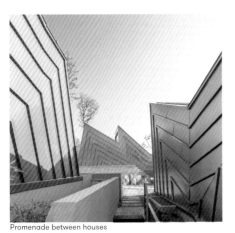
Promenade between houses

Site plan

N   0 5   15   25m

Side view of a house in the compound

Gate pavilion at entrance

View of road in the middle area of the site

Upper dining room and lower living room beyond

View of upper study room from lower living room

Stairs to upper dining room and lower family room

View of living room from upper study room

Upper dining room

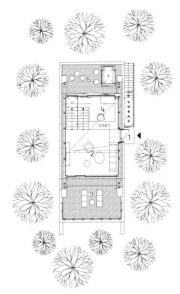

Basement plan of A-type house

First-floor plan of A-type house

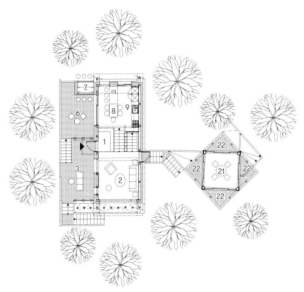

Basement plan of B1- and B2-type house

First-floor plan of B1- and B2-type house

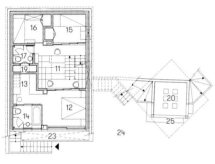

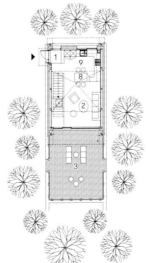

1.   Entrance
2.   Living room
3.   Living room terrace
4.   Study
5.   Study terrace
6.   Dining terrace
7.   Toplight/outdoor table
8.   Dining room
9.   Kitchen
10. Family room
11. Stairs in family room
12. Main bedroom
13. Dressing room
14. Main bathroom
15. Bedroom 1
16. Bedroom 2
17. Bathroom
18. Dining garden
19. Boiler room
20. Pavilion
21. Guestroom
22. Terrace
23. Main bedroom garden
24. Garden
25. Veranda

Basement plan of C-type house

First-floor plan of C-type house

Main bedroom in basement

Family room in basement

Main bedroom in basement

Road view from lower area of site

Front elevation of A-type house

Front elevation of B2-type house

Front elevation of C-type house

Left side elevation of B2-type house

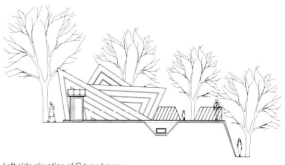

Left side elevation of C-type house

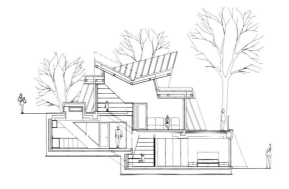

Sections of A-type house

Section of B1-type house

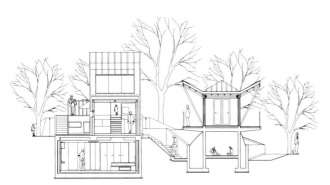
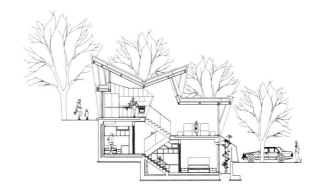

Sections of B2-type house

Section of C-type house

Dining room and outdoor garden beyond

Upper dining room and lower study room

Northern perspective

Architect firm: Tongji Architectural Design (Group) Co., Ltd (TJAD)
Principal architect: Ren Lizhi
Design team: Chen Xianglei, Zheng Yimin, Liu Jin, Qian Bihua, Jin Hai
Location: Beijing, China
Area: 35,625 square meters
Completion date: August 2014
Photography: ZY Studio, Lv Hengzhong

The new campus library of Beijing University of Civil Engineering and Architecture is located in the central area of the campus and houses the university's own existing library, as well as the state-supported China Architecture Library.

Located at the center of the central axis of the campus, the library fulfills core view demands and is visible from all directions of the orthogonal campus network. Pure geometric forms are used to abstractly represent the significance of the building as the core of the campus, being positioned at the center of it.

A highly centralized design strategy establishes an inherent culture-carrying characteristic in the library, as a spacious multilevel landscape space in front of the library enables the extension and penetration of the surrounding academic atmosphere.

The GRC (glass fiber-reinforced-concrete) grid cladding on the upper façade of the building integrates an abstract illustration of the "five elements" in traditional Chinese belief—wood, fire, earth, water, and metal—as it complies to functional shading requirements on different orientations. The building skin abstractly provides a modern interpretation of traditional hollow lattice windows, deriving new forms and meanings in this design. The skin grid is repeated in 4.2-by-2.1-meter modules to form a rhombus-shaped basic skeleton; the warping is made in a quantitative way based on the light requirements, which is controlled within nine types of unit modules to reduce costs. The non-linear curved shape of the bottom of the building is realized by using a special curved steel furnace processing technology that can change in multiple directions.

The coffee lounge, exhibition space, and academic salon migrate the focus of the library beyond just centering on book collections to include people orientation, cooperation, and communication. The spiral staircase in the atrium connects the reading space seamlessly, satisfying both purposeful book-locating or non-specific browsing—in which case, visitors can either access materials in a targeted manner, or get

inspired by the collections on the shelves as they wander through the aisles.

Unlike the one-way transfer of knowledge in traditional libraries, the new library pays more attention to information sharing and communication, and provides a variety of places that can meet different learning styles, from collaborative work to quiet learning. To facilitate this, a flexible information sharing space around the atrium, a semi-open reading space combined with a side atrium, and a small independent study space on the top floor have been included in the program. Reading rooms with various themes are also integrated on different reading floors in a relaxed and flexible spiral layout.

The library also features eco-friendly features in its design, such as energy-saving and emission-reducing systems that enhance environmental benefits: the waterscape on the north side establishes a suitable microclimate; the double skin effectively provides shading function; the high central atrium combines with the surrounding side atrium to channel airflow; and the skylights placed in the atrium provide sufficient natural light within the interior.

Bird's-eye view

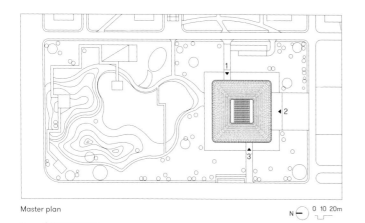

Master plan

N ⊕ 0 10 20m

1.   Office entrance
2.   Main entrance
3.   Lecture hall entrance

Southwestern perspective

Reading area in atrium

Side open space in reading area

Atrium

Conference area

View of the shared hall from the stairs

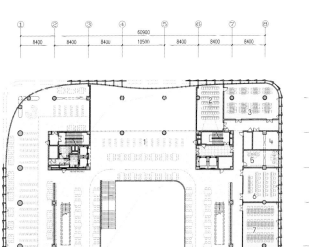

1. New books display
2. Projector room
3. Audiovisual room
4. Air conditioner room
5. Administration office
6. Audiovisual collection room
7. Reading room—electronic collection
8. Public reading space
9. TU catalog
10. Rest area
11. Design and cultural creation venue
12. Teacher's library

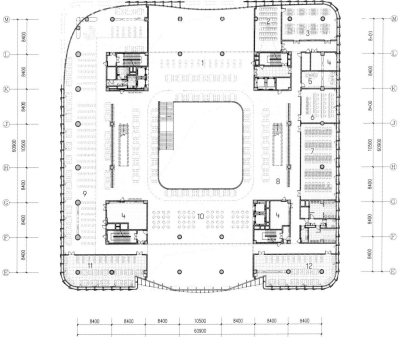

Second-floor plan

1. Lecture hall lobby
2. Café
3. Temporary exhibition and rest area
4. Public access catalog area
5. Reception
6. Office lobby
7. Library services hall
8. Library services reception
9. Air conditioner room
10. Book reservation room
11. Temporary storeroom
12. Fire protection control room and security
    monitoring station
13. Office
14. Acquisition, editing, and processing room
15. Restroom
16. Storeroom
17. Printing service
18. Self-service book return
19. Public access catalog area
20. Bookstore
21. Secondary entrance to lecture hall
22. Main entrance
23. Secondary entrance to logistics area
24. Water landscape

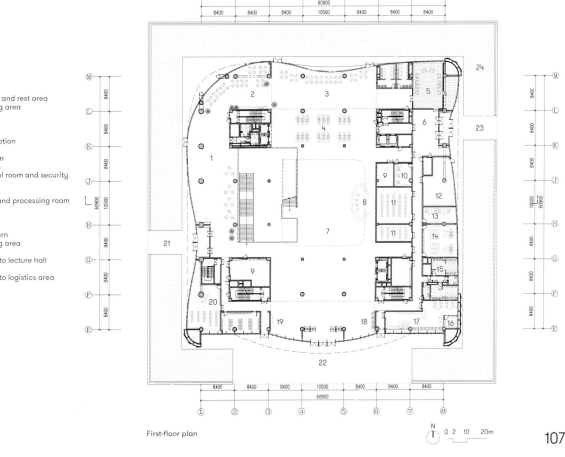

First-floor plan

N   0 2 10   20m

Northwestern perspective

Plan sections

4F

7F

3F

6F

2F

5F

1F

TONGJI
ARCHITECTURAL DESIGN
(GROUP) CO., LTD.

Exterior of the TJAD office building

ABOUT TJAD

Tongji Architectural Design (Group) Co., Ltd. (TJAD), formerly known as the Architectural Design and Research Institute of Tongji University, was founded in 1958 and has now developed into a well-known large-scale design and consulting group.

Shanghai Museum East Hall

With almost seventy years of history behind them, and with the profound cultural foundation of Tongji University, TJAD has accumulated a rich experience in both engineering design and technical consultancy, progressing notably over the last sixty-four years. TJAD is a design institution with one of the most extensive design qualifications in China, with a business scope that includes consulting, engineering design, project management, geotechnical engineering, and geological exploration in the fields of building engineering, road engineering, municipal engineering, landscape engineering, environmental pollution prevention, and conservation of historical and cultural relics, among others. The organization has embarked on thousands of projects in China, Africa, and South America that include, among many, Shanghai Tower, Fangfei Garden of the Diaoyutai State Guest House, Table Tennis Gymnasium of the 2008 Olympic Games, African Union Conference Center, New Jinggangshan Revolution Museum, Shanghai Xintiandi, Theme Pavilion of the 2010 Shanghai Expo, Shanghai International Tourist Resort, Shanghai Natural History Museum, Shanghai Symphony Orchestra Concert Hall, China Corporate United Pavilion of Expo 2015 Milan, Havana Hotel of Cuba, Saikang Di Stadium of the Republic of Ghana, the National Arts Center of Republic of Trinidad and Tobago, Sutong Yangtze River Highway Bridge, and Shanghai A5 (Jiading-Jinshan) Expressway Project.

Shanghai Tower
(Cooperative Design,
in partnership with
Gensler, Cosentini, and
Thornton Tomasetti)

Museum of Art Pudong
(Cooperative Design,
in partnership with
Ateliers Jean Nouvel)

Xi'an International Convention and Exhibition Center (Cooperative Design, in partnership with gmp and WES)

TJAD employs more than five thousand outstanding architectural design and engineering personnel to provide top engineering consulting services for our clients, and we have been working hard to promote urban development, so that we may build a better life for citizens through our many professional practices.

We firmly believe that it is the trust that our clients have in us that gives TJAD opportunities to grow. As part of the society and industry, we strive to continue to channel unremitting efforts toward industry development and social progress, just like we have been doing the past sixty-four years.

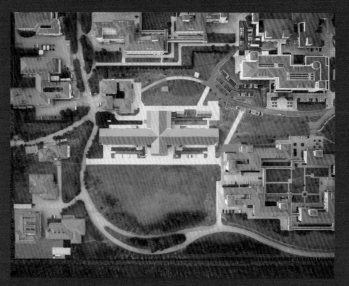

Contingency and Temporary Medical Building of Shanghai Public Health Clinical Center

Shangyin Opera House (Cooperative Design, in partnership with Christian de Portzamparc, Xu-Acoustique, and Theater Projects Consultants)

Green Hill, Shanghai

TONGJI ARCHITECTURAL DESIGN (GROUP) CO., LTD., (TJAD)

VISION

Become a respected design and engineering consultancy with global influence

MISSION

Enable people to live and work in a better place with our creative labor

CORE VALUES

Focus on customers and grow together with employees

SPIRIT

Work together and pursue excellence

Address: No.1230 Siping Road, Shanghai, China, 200092

Telephone: 0086-21-65987788

Email: 5wjia@tjad.cn

Web: www.tjad.cn